WRITING FOR RADIO

Rosemary Horstmann

A & C Black · London

First published 1988
A & C Black (Publishers) Ltd
35 Bedford Row, London WC1R 4JH

© 1988 Rosemary Horstmann

ISBN 0 7136 3008 6

British Library Cataloguing in Publication Data
Horstmann, Rosemary
 Writing for radio.
  1. Radio programmes. Scripts. Composition
  I. Title.
  808'.066
 ISBN 0–7136–3008–6

Typeset by Latimer Trend & Company Ltd, Plymouth
Printed in Great Britain by
Whitstable Litho Ltd, Whitstable, Kent

Contents

Foreword

Some readers of this book may already be established writers, perhaps seeking the challenge of a new market; others may never have seriously set pen to paper before. It is never too late to start – there is no age barrier to writing and broadcasting, and no sex barrier either. I hope, however, that many will be standing on the threshold of working life and considering the possibility of a career in broadcasting, particularly in radio. For radio is an important medium in its own right, not to be regarded merely as television without the pictures.

Would-be radio professionals should appreciate that broadcasters fall into two main categories: those who plan or produce programmes and so commission writers and performers, and those who do the writing and performing. People in the first category tend to hold staff appointments; those in the second are almost invariably freelances. The salaried producer or executive may count on a steady job with a pay cheque at the end of the month, and a pension when he retires (and here I should make it clear that throughout this book 'he' means 'he' or 'she'). On the other hand, his voice will seldom be heard, and the public will remain largely unaware of his existence. He is an *eminence grise* behind the scenes, holding the purse strings and dispensing patronage.

The life of the freelance is more glamorous and more chancy. If he does well he will earn far more than the producers who commission him. A successful radio personality can make an international name for himself. But he has no job security, and is always dependent on the goodwill of those who control the broadcasting machine to go on booking him. Schedules alter, producers move, tastes change. It is a truism of the freelance life that you are either overworked or starving.

With the exception of announcers and newsreaders most of the people whose voices you hear day by day are freelances. They may be retained on long-term contracts or booked *ad hoc* for each broadcast, but they are all subject to the hazards of show-business life. For that, after all, is what broadcasting is – a branch of the entertainments industry.

What does a producer do? He is an ideas merchant and his job is to fill air-time in a way which will attract listeners. He buys talent, in the form of writers and performers, and works with them to develop and polish their creative efforts. In film and television the functions of producer and director are divided, but in radio the producer is usually his own director. This means that, having commissioned or bought a script and chosen the performers, he then goes into the studio and directs the recording. He understands the medium of radio, knows the audience he is trying to reach, and helps the broadcaster to present himself and his material as effectively as possible, first by editing the script, and then by guiding the performance.

There are many other tasks in broadcasting besides producing and performing. Every station has to have engineers, administrators and accountants. If it is a commercial station it will have a sales section. Depending on the scale of the operation, there will be secretaries, telephonists, receptionists, perhaps a librarian, certainly press and public relations staff. If you are drawn to this crazy, stimulating world, one way in is to get yourself a job – any job – at a radio station, in order to watch the wheels go round, make contacts, and convince people that you are genuine in your determination to break into the competitive business of broadcasting. If you have taken a hand in school or college productions or helped with a hospital broadcasting station this will stand you in good stead.

It is hard to make a living as a freelance, especially in the early stages. Any writer needs to find a way of supporting himself while he works at his creative calling in leisure hours, until he becomes sufficiently well-established to be able to give the job up and write full-time. Constant rejection is disheartening, and the most valuable quality to cultivate is thick-skinned persistence. Analyse the reasons for the rejection of your efforts, and keep on trying. I hope this book will help, and that eventually you will win through to the happy situation of being paid for what you enjoy doing – and what can be more rewarding than that?

Introduction:
The Nature of Radio

Radio has been with us since the beginning of the century. In Britain the first regular service of radio programmes for the general public was started in 1922, more than sixty years ago. Many things have changed since then. I can remember my grandfather sitting with headphones over his ears beside an enormous and mysterious black box with glowing glass bulbs on top. What he was listening to I never knew. Perhaps it was one of Sir Walford Davies's early talks on music; it might even have been the first radio play, broadcast in 1924. Whatever it was, the signal reached his receiver, with its glimmering valves, by means of a wire which led out of the window and across the garden to the top of a tall flag-pole. This elaborate aerial array was an essential part of the paraphernalia. The ritual of Grandpa listening to the wireless had more than a touch of the ceremonial, like some arcane religious observance. Woe betide us children if our clumsy footsteps should shake the delicate connections or disturb the fine tuning. Once while he was sitting rapt in some communication from the unknown my two-year old sister dealt Grandpa a smart blow on his bald head with a walking stick. He leapt to his feet convinced the set had been struck by lightning.

The pole at the bottom of the garden disappeared long ago, but headphones, having ceased to be essential, have now made a come-back as part of the new mobility of radio. Today people no longer have to sit beside the receiver. Liberated by the transistor and the battery from the tyranny of trailing cables they can listen to the American President addressing a press conference in the White House as they ride to work in the train, or enjoy their favourite pop programme as they jog round the park. This universal accessibility makes radio unique as a means of communication.

Since the 1940s television has gradually taken over the limelight. Television is expensive, sensational, glamorous. But radio remains a highly significant element in the world's mass media. Although it no longer makes headlines, even in a television-rich country like Britain there are few who do not listen to the radio at least once a day, and a shut-down in radio services would bring far more universal consternation than a shut-down in television.

Radio is cheap. It can span vast distances in the twinkling of an eye, and because, unlike television, it does not demand a reliable electricity supply it can be used with confidence to reach isolated communities and individuals beyond the range of piped power, whether in remote moorland farmsteads, in ships at sea, or the Australian outback. Here we come to the first significant point for the writer to remember about radio broadcasting.

We call it a mass medium, and it is true that its audiences are counted in millions. But they are millions of individuals, sitting in ones and twos by their own firesides, or listening in their cars or out on their farms and cattle-stations. The style in which they like to be addressed is an intimate one, not at all the same manner as they would expect at a public meeting. The broadcaster is only as far from his audience as his mouth is from the microphone and his listener's chair is from the loudspeaker at the other end.

The second important point is that the listener is for all practical purposes blind. The broadcaster's message must reach him through one sense only, the sense of hearing. This is not to say that the contributions to total experience made by the other four senses should be ignored. Rather, the writer must cunningly incorporate these contributions in his work. Choice of the right words will enable the listener to see, touch, smell and even taste – in his imagination. It is this skill of stimulating the imagination that lies at the heart of the radio writer's art.

The ordinary writer starts with a sheet of blank paper; the radio writer starts with silence. Every sound that is added to that silence will carry some clue, which the audience will be waiting, 'all ears', to interpret. The very quality of the acoustic will convey something of the location in which words are spoken. A religious service relayed from a cathedral sounds quite different from a studio broadcast. Practitioners of radio drama know well how to exploit these subtleties, and an accompaniment of exotic background noises adds an invaluable touch of authenticity to news reports from remote corners of the earth.

Thirdly, the radio writer must never forget that his listeners are bound to take in his message sequentially, in the order in which he gives it to them. If they do not immediately understand what has been said, they cannot look back to the beginning of the paragraph, or re-read the previous page as one can with print. For most listeners the first hearing is the last, and anything misunderstood or missed is gone for ever. Hence, it is essential for the writer to structure his message carefully with this limitation in mind, and to have a clear mental image of the people for whom he is writing.

The key points made in this introduction are valid for every type of radio programme, and should never be forgotten. Radio is an intimate medium, carrying its message to millions of individuals through their ears alone. Listeners have to accept broadcast information in the sequence in which it is presented. Clarity of thought and empathy with the audience are the marks of the successful radio writer.

1
The Organisation
of Broadcasting

World broadcasting has been characterised as falling into three main categories: permissive – you give the public what it wants; paternalistic – you give it what you think it ought to want; and authoritarian – you give it what the government wants. The last category manifests itself in totalitarian regimes, such as the USSR. The second is typified by British broadcasting, and the first by the American approach. In the USA radio, and later television, have always been regarded as part of the business system, to be financed by revenue from advertising and sponsorship. Only comparatively recently has a need been recognised for public broadcasting as an alternative to the commercial service. The early 1920s saw a free-for-all boom in American radio that led to chaos on the air waves, and it was primarily this rather than distaste for advertising that led the British government to insist on strict regulation and, for the first fifty years, no advertising.

Birth of British broadcasting

Broadcasting in Britain started with the BBC. The British Broadcasting Corporation (formerly the British Broadcasting Company) received a Royal Charter in 1927. Its first Director General, John Reith (later Lord Reith), was a visionary of towering personality and unswerving rectitude. He believed that the BBC had a duty to inform, educate and entertain its audience to the highest standards, and under his guidance a tradition of public service broadcasting was created against which all later developments have come to be measured.

The BBC was given a monopoly of the British air waves. It was to be financed by a licence fee paid by the audience, and was forbidden to accept money for advertising. The King in Council was to appoint a Board of Governors, who would in turn appoint the Director General responsible to them for the running of the Corporation. Subject to the law of the land, the BBC was to be free of detailed control over the content of its programmes. The Government would, however, retain a right of veto over the broadcasting of any material which was felt to be against the national interest, and the BBC could also be required to broadcast official announcements. In 1937, when the first Royal Charter was renewed, the BBC was given responsibility for television as well as radio, and also authorised to broadcast 'for the benefit of Our dominions beyond the seas and territories under Our protection' — the Empire Service, which became the World Service.

The Fourth Charter was granted in 1952. The Government had 'come to the conclusion that in the expanding field of television provision should be made to permit some element of competition.' Accordingly, the BBC's licence to broadcast was for the first time described as non-exclusive. This paved the way for the breaking of the BBC's monopoly with the launching of Independent Television, later to be joined by Independent Local Radio.

During the sixty years that have elapsed since the granting of the first Charter and Licence the BBC has jealously guarded its independence from Government control. Its policy of absolute impartiality and objectivity in the handling of news and controversial issues has brought it a world-wide reputation which British governments of all political colours regard as a national asset. The Corporation has acted responsibly so that the Government has never felt compelled to invoke its power of veto, even in times of war and national crisis. Should the BBC be required by the Home Secretary to broadcast an official announcement against its will, it reserves the right to state that the transmission is being made under Government orders. In practice this has never been necessary, as such announcements normally make news, and are covered as such in the regular news output. Other countries find it hard to believe that the BBC is truly independent, and indeed the Corporation walks a delicate tightrope in its handling of news and current affairs. Nevertheless, anything that looks like an attempt by the government of the day to interfere in BBC output is greeted with storms of indignation in parliament and the press, where the BBC is hotly defended as a flagship of free speech.

Radio in the Commonwealth

The British way of broadcasting was growing up at the same time as the British Empire was dissolving. One by one the colonies became independent nations, and imperial bonds were transmuted into the looser links of Commonwealth. As the patches of red drained from the map and the Empire builders withdrew they left behind many legacies, of which two concern this book. The English language became a world *lingua franca* through which people living in scattered communities who spoke different languages — and different dialects of the same language – could talk to each other and be understood. The second legacy was the idea of broadcasting as a public service. Even where commercial radio and television have come to exist side by side with a national service, as they have in Britain, this concept continues to permeate broadcasting throughout the former British Empire.

For example, All India Radio from its headquarters in New Delhi, operates a broadcasting network of 86 centres, covering all the important cultural and linguistic regions of that vast sub-continent. Its programmes consist of music, talks, plays, discussions, interviews, special programmes for women and children, schools and universities, and rural broadcasts for community listening. All India Radio is a department of the Ministry of Information and Broadcasting, and is funded nationally. It has all the characteristics of an Asian BBC. A commercial radio service was introduced in 1967, from AIR Bombay-Pune-Nagpur, and this has now been considerably extended.

In Africa, broadcasting holds a position of overwhelming importance among the public media. Radio, above all, is the only medium which can overcome the barriers of illiteracy, distance, and lack of transportation. Unfortunately the trend in Africa has been towards the authoritarian pattern, and in spite of high ideals on the part of individuals, broadcasting tends to be under direct government control, and closely involved with politics.

BBC domestic services

Today the BBC is a vast organisation employing tens of thousands both in London and at its regional and local production centres throughout the United Kingdom. As far as radio is concerned it is responsible for four national networks. These have each developed a clearly defined character, but according to a discussion document recently issued by the BBC there are likely to be some shifts of emphasis in the 1990s.

Radio 1 has established an image as the channel for young listeners, with pop music, DJ chat and some news, while Radio 2 is regarded as easy listening for the over-25s. The BBC proposes to improve the public service component on both these channels by increasing the number of informational campaigns, and to include elements of drama, documentary and specialist music, and possibly part of the educational output.

Radio 3 will continue to be the nation's premier cultural service on radio, while Radio 4 will be maintained and developed as the primary national information and speech network.

Programmes may be contributed to these main networks by

producers working in any of the BBC's regional production centres. Transmitters in the regions – especially the three national Regions, Wales, Scotland and Northern Ireland – frequently opt out of the main Radio 4 network to broadcast separate programmes of local interest.

In addition to its four main networks broadcast nationwide, the BBC also has more than forty Local Radio Stations. These are stations with limited-power transmitters, designed to serve the particular needs and interests of listeners living in their immediate areas.

All the BBC's domestic services are paid for from the television licence fee. There is no separate licence for radio sets. Nearly two-thirds of the UK population listen to BBC radio at some time or another during the week. Typical audiences for current popular programmes are:

> Top 40 (Radio 1) 4,900,000
> Jimmy Young (Radio 2) 2,200,000
> Your Concert Choice (Radio 3) 100,000
> The Archers Omnibus (Radio 4) 1,000,000

BBC External Services

These include the World Service in English and overseas foreign language services, both financed by grant-in-aid from the Treasury. They estimate the size of their regular audience world-wide as about 100 million adults, not including China. The BBC World Service broadcasts in English 24 hours a day. In addition, news and current affairs coverage is transmitted in a range of foreign tongues, which have included over fifty different languages since the service started in 1938.

The headquarters of the BBC External Services at Bush House in London is a miniature BBC in itself. It has a similar range of departments, and although it takes a good deal of material from the BBC's domestic services freelances should remember that it also originates many programmes itself, specially designed for its overseas audiences. The emphasis in the External Services output is on accurate and unbiased news and information, projection of British culture, and education. 'English by Radio' has been an overwhelming success, and BBC English-teaching programmes are now heard or seen in more than 120 countries all over the world.

The BBC Transcription Service, part of the External Services, places recorded programmes on the domestic networks of over 100 different countries, thus overcoming problems of audibility. This department is also responsible for the Topical Tapes service, which supplies up-to-date news and documentary programmes for local transmission. Most of these have already been broadcast in other services of the BBC, but the Topical Tapes Unit does originate some of its own material.

The External Services are also responsible for the BBC's Monitoring Service, based at Caversham near Reading, where foreign radio broadcasts are listened to and reported.

More than 80 other countries support broadcasting services addressed to listeners outside their national boundaries. At the top of the league table in 1986 was the USA, with Voice of America, Radio Free Europe, Radio Liberty and Radio Marti putting out nearly 2500 hours per week between them. The USSR was a close second with about 2300 hours, and third came China with some 1450 hours. The German Federal Republic was in fourth place with 821 hours, and Britain's BBC came fifth with 733 hours.

Commercial radio

The BBC monopoly in radio was challenged from the beginning by Radio Normandy and Radio Luxembourg, commercial stations broadcasting from the continent of Europe. Radio Normandy did not survive the Second World War, but Radio Luxembourg is still going strong, and has extended its interests to include television. Its assault on the British air waves was joined in the 1960s by 'pirate' radio stations such as Radio Caroline, operating from a ship in the Thames Estuary, and offering a diet of pop music and disc-jockey chat. Clearly there was a demand for different sorts of radio, and in 1973 the first legitimate commercial stations were launched in mainland Britain.

The Independent Television Authority, renamed the Independent Broadcasting Authority, was given responsibility for overseeing commercial radio. The advent of advertising was strictly regulated. Applicants for franchises had to convince the IBA that their programme plans would provide an acceptable standard of service for each local community involved. It was forbidden to integrate advertising into programme content, and the commercials themselves were to be clearly segregated. Sponsorship was forbidden, except under the strictest rules. Recently there has been a re-think on this. With the rise of independent production houses, largely stimulated by the advent of Channel 4 Television, the need to find new ways of funding broadcast programmes, especially on the arts, has led to the conclusion that discreet commercial sponsorship can be perfectly acceptable. This view now has official blessing, not only for IBA but also for BBC programmes when commissioned from independent producers. There are now some fifty ILR (Independent Local Radio) stations in operation, and a certain amount of programme exchange goes on between them, facilitated by AIRC, the Association of Independent Radio Contractors. The tradition of public service is maintained in the Independent sector, as in BBC local radio, although the stations vary a good deal in the style and content of their programming. Independent Radio News (a subsidiary of the London ILR station LBC) provides a news service to ILR stations throughout the country, and standards of balance, accuracy and impartiality are scrupulously maintained.

British Forces Broadcasting Service

One other British broadcasting organisation deserves mention here – the British Forces Broadcasting Service, radio arm of the Services Sound and Vision Corporation. Its role is to provide a service for the British forces overseas, encompassing entertainment, information and education, together with a link with home. BFBS Radio operates stations in Germany, Cyprus, Gibraltar, Hong Kong, Brunei, the Falklands and Belize, which devise their own programme schedules to suit the needs and interests of their audiences, drawing on local contributions as well as material supplied by London. BFBS HQ in London does not transmit live, but records over 50 hours of programmes every week in a wide range of speech and music. These are syndicated to overseas stations. In addition, up to 30 Royal Navy ships at sea regularly receive a large proportion of BFBS London's output every week. Recently, satellite transmission has made it possible to hook up direct with all the main overseas BFBS stations, and broadcast 24 hours a day, with up-to-date news on the hour and sometimes on the half hour as well. Sports commentaries are particularly appreciated by the service audience overseas. The Services Sound and Vision Corporation is a registered charity, and any profits are split 50/50 between improving the service and the various benevolent funds. A special agreement on copyright has been negotiated with the Performing Rights Society, on condition that none of the BFBS output is ever heard in Britain.

Many changes are in prospect for radio in Britain. A broadcasting bill is expected in the near future which will give the go-ahead for up to three independent national radio channels, together with another tier of broadcasting at low-power level – community radio. It has not yet been decided how community radio stations are to be financed, or whether they will be regulated tightly or not at all. One thing is clear – radio broadcasting is far from dying of old age. In fact it looks as if it is in for a renaissance in which the skills of presenters, writers, and broadcasters of all kinds will be more in demand than ever.

2
Writing for Speech

Words, words, words! Writers use words to communicate messages in print; radio writers use words designed to be lifted off the page and spoken aloud. In this chapter we shall try to discover some of the differences between the two.

If you listen to people talking to each other in a bus or a train you will notice that their use of language is somewhat casual and untidy. In ordinary conversation people pause, stumble, and pick themselves up. They speak in short phrases and incomplete sentences as the thoughts come into their minds. They repeat words although the sense does not require it; they don't try to find different words to avoid overworking the same ones; and even educated people can be very ungrammatical in conversation.

Consider two reports of the same event, first as you might read it in a local newspaper:

TEENAGER FEARED KIDNAPPED

Police fear that pretty dark-haired Mary Smith who failed to return from shopping on Saturday afternoon may have been kidnapped. Wearing a fluorescent red anorak and boots she was last seen by school friend Joan Brown in Ambridge High Street at 3.15 pm. Joan says 'She was going to buy a skirt and then go home. She is not the sort of girl to do anything silly. I hope nothing dreadful has happened to her!' Police enquiries are continuing.

Now listen to Joan Brown talking to a friend on the telephone:

Hallo! Betty! Can you hear me? This is an awful line. Listen – a dreadful thing has happened. You know Mary Smith? The dark girl with curly hair? She's disappeared – gone missing! I saw her in the High Street on Saturday afternoon. She was wearing a new anorak – said her mother had given it to her for Christmas. Bright red, it was – what do they call it? Fluorescent. She was hunting for a skirt to go with it. Then she was going to get the bus home. But she never arrived! They're saying on the radio she's been kidnapped. Isn't it awful?

The structure of each of these reports is quite different. The newspaper report is impersonal and factual, and packs in everything possible at the beginning. The reporter has written it in such a way that the sub-editor can cut it from the end, and even if he only has room for one sentence the story is there. The sensational headline tells all, even if hurried readers merely glance at the page. But just try reading that paragraph aloud! People do not talk like that.

Now compare the telephone conversation. First, Joan makes sure her friend is listening and gives her a teaser to heighten the suspense. With her listener hooked she then tells her story in short bursts, one scrap of information at a time, building it phrase by phrase to a climax. Joan has a proper sense of drama and has, in fact, produced the microcosm of a successful radio talk. Incidentally, she has also followed the journalistic maxim 'Tell them what you're going to tell them, then tell them, then tell them you've told them'. Skilful writing for speech, however, means more than just transcribing the normal features of everyday conversation. It is question of combining careful structure and imaginative use of language with an effect of spontaneity.

Scripted discussion

In the early days of radio, when the authorities were afraid of letting anyone loose on the air without a script and tape-editing was unheard-of, there was a programme format called the 'scripted discussion'. Three or four speakers would be brought together with a chairman in a studio to talk about the subject of the proposed broadcast. The conversation would be recorded and then transcribed, word for word. This was called 'telediphoning', and usually it yielded an astonishingly unreadable result. The producer would sit down with the transcript and edit it into a tidy, logical well-structured script without 'ers' and 'I means' and 'you knows', in which all the desired points were properly brought out. Finally the participants would be brought to the studio again to read the scripted version of their own words, and this would be broadcast live as a 'spontaneous' discussion.

The trouble with this technique was that speakers were being asked to behave like actors. Many people can talk with animation on a topic they feel strongly about, but it takes skill and practice to read dialogue convincingly from a script, even if the words were your own in the first place. The scripted discussion format produced some flat and stilted results and was soon abandoned.

Scripted talks

The scripted talk, however, is still very much alive, and the technique of recording and transcribing your own words is a useful one in drafting a script you are going to deliver yourself. You will have to be prepared to do this if you are putting forward your own views or

describing a personal experience. In general, broadcasting organisa-
tions do not buy talks scripts from one person to be read by another.
Listeners like to feel that they are meeting, over the air, the actual
person who climbed the mountain, broke the speed record, objects
strongly to the new law, or has personal expertise in putting new
washers on taps – whatever the subject may be. Short stories are a
different matter, but more of that later.

Listen to yourself on a tape recorder. The experience of hearing
yourself recorded for the first time is usually unpleasant. Who is this
stranger with the funny squeaky voice and the appalling vowels? Do
you really sound like that? Your friends assure you it is exactly like
you, just as they do when they show you an unflattering snapshot. It is
a curious fact that the microphone seems to exaggerate individual
vocal traits. You will never before have heard your voice as others hear
it, because in the ordinary way it reverberates inside your head as well
as coming to your ears across an air gap. But this stranger is the person
your audience will meet. If you are to write successfully for yourself
you must study your own style of speech, come to terms with your
own vocal personality, and construct the sort of sentences that will sit
easily on your tongue.

Don't worry if a foreign or regional accent is more marked than you
had believed, provided you can be clearly understood. It is probably
what gives your way of speech its special character. Time was when
non-standard English would have been considered a disadvantage, but
nowadays for all except would-be newsreaders and announcers a
foreign or regional flavour in the voice can be a distinct asset. Think of
the many top broadcasters with an Irish brogue! Thick dialect can be
hard to understand for those unfamiliar with it, and this has to be
watched, but the odd dialect word or expression can bring vitality to
an otherwise bland script.

One of the most successful practitioners of the broadcast talk was
the writer J.B. Priestley. He had a warm, friendly vocal personality,
with a strong flavour of his native Yorkshire, and the seven-minute
'Postscripts' that he broadcast on Sunday evenings after the nine
o'clock news during the first summer of the war in 1940 are classics of
the medium. They drew such a response from listeners that they were
published in book form, with a preface by Priestley himself. He points
out that they were 'meant to be spoken and heard over the air and not
to be read in cold print ... wireless talks and not essays'. Two
important conclusions emerged, he said, from his experience of
broadcasting these Postscripts:

The first, and less important, is the immense, the staggering power and
effect of broadcasting...as a medium of communication broadcasting

makes everything else seem like the method of a secret society. So long as you don't go on too long and the listeners are not tired of you, a mere whisper over the air seems to start an avalanche. Mention a couple of ducks and they are photographed as if they were film stars. Refer to a pie in a shop window, and instantly there are pilgrimages to it. . . .

The second and more important conclusion that emerges from this short chapter of broadcasting experience is that. . .what holds the attention of most decent folk is a genuine sharing of feelings and views on the part of the broadcaster. He must talk as if he were among serious friends, and not as if he had suddenly been appointed head of an infants' school. People may be almost inarticulate themselves, and yet recognise in an instant when something that is at least trying to be real and true is being said to them.

Much of Priestley's success was due to the fact that he did not 'read' to the microphone; he talked to it. If you are to be a successful broadcaster you must learn to read your own words as if they had just come into your mind. So use the tape recorder as a means of drafting your talk. Write out exactly what you said, and then edit and re-organise it. Resist the temptation to condense the sentences and tidy them up. Leave in the repetitions and the short uneven phrases. Consider the punctuation: punctuation for speech is different from punctuation for print. In speech it is used more like the dynamic signs in music. You will need more commas to mark the phrases, and a liberal use of dashes can be helpful.

Your talk will be intended for a particular broadcasting slot, so you will write with a specific length in mind. A page of A4 typescript in double spacing will take about two minutes to read aloud — roughly 140 words a minute, depending on the sort of material and the way you talk. Work with a stop-watch, and tailor your script carefully for length. If your draft is too long, prune it by taking out whole sentences or paragraphs rather than condensing it by means of subordinate clauses. Don't be tempted into believing that you can shorten it by speaking faster. Remember, also, that when you are 'talking' aloud from a script you will automatically read more slowly than when you are reading silently to yourself.

Identify the boring words and look for vivid expressions to substitute for them — words that will conjure up pictures in your listeners' minds. Remember you need to make them hear, smell, and feel as well as see. Keep the personal sense of involvement always alive before them. Not 'Egypt is hot in July', but 'I was sweating in the humid Egyptian summer'. Brian Hanrahan gave a classic demonstration of this in a famous despatch during the Falklands War. He was describing an air strike from a British carrier, and was not allowed to give details of the forces involved. Instead of saying 'Our aircraft suffered no losses', he said 'I counted them all out and I counted them all back' – and in imagination his listeners stood on the deck with him.

If you need to put over facts and figures which may be difficult for a listener to grasp, try to put the information in an easily understandable way. For example, instead of giving measurements and figures use a simile such as 'the size of a tennis court' or 'enough people to fill Wembley Stadium'. If it is essential for precise details to be conveyed, for example the quantities in a cookery recipe, suggest at the start that your listeners have pencil and paper handy so that you can repeat the ingredients slowly at the end of your talk, or give an address where people can write for a handout.

A word of warning about humour and irony. Remember that your audience cannot see your facial expression. 'A smile in the voice' is something skilled broadcasters know how to achieve, but it takes practice, and in its absence listeners may easily misunderstand the spirit of some dryly witty comment.

When you have made your script as effective as you know how, type it out, in double spacing on one side of the paper only, and send it with a short covering letter to the producer of the programme to which you want to contribute. You can, if you like, send a cassette as well, to give the producer an idea of your vocal personality. This cassette will almost certainly not be broadcast. Instead, if your script is liked, you will be invited to go to the studio and record it, or perhaps broadcast it 'live'. More guidance on submitting scripts and ideas is given in Chapter 12 on Markets, Fees and Copyright.

Short stories

It may be that you want to write short stories for radio. In this case, your script will probably be given to someone else to read – unless, that is, you are a professional actor yourself. The standard BBC slot for short stories is fifteen minutes long, which means about 2500 words. The important thing here is to create characters that an actor can bring to life in his performance. First person stories, in which the tale is told by a clearly characterised narrator, are often particularly successful, and it is wise in any case to confine yourself to one person's viewpoint. It may help to think of a short story as a play for one voice.

The opening of a short story is crucial. Within the first few moments the audience has to 'tune in' to the voice and character of the narrator, and decide whether or not to go on listening. It is important, however, not to give a piece of information that is vital to the enjoyment of the rest of the story in the very first sentence. People switch on late, and often for a variety of reasons fail to register the first few words. Arouse the listener's curiosity with an intriguing opening, offer him believable characters which can be brought to life by a skilled reader, and round your story off with a satisfying end. Although many short stories have a twist in the tail this is by no means essential, so long as the end feels 'right' to the listener.

The BBC's main short story slot at present is on Radio 4 at 10.30 in the morning. Other radio stations, such as LBC, broadcast them in the middle of the night, for the benefit of shift workers and insomniacs. The mood of an audience changes subtly over the twenty-four hours, and broadcasters learn how to take this into account in scheduling and manner of presentation.

Continuity and presentation

Each network has its own individual style, and it is quite possible to tell from the sound of a channel, before you have distinguished a single word or heard a station identification, which one you are listening to. Brash, brisk Radio 1 contrasts sharply with the more easy-going approach of Radio 2, while the long-winded, scholarly announcements which preface programmes on Radio 3 are quite different from the straightforward, journalistic presentation on Radio 4. Local radio stations also each have their own 'house style', on which they have built their listening figures. Writing continuity and announcements for each station calls for a different approach, in tune with the expectations of the audience. We come back to one of the key points made at the beginning of this book: empathy with the audience is a key ingredient in successful broadcasting.

3
Using Actuality:
Tape Recording and
Editing

You may assume that as a radio-writer it is your job simply to provide a script and record some interviews with interesting people, and that a helpful technician will then edit your material and put it in order for you to introduce in the studio. Time was when this was true. Nowadays, however, highly-paid technical assistance is at a premium, and time in a professional editing suite is expensive. You will stand a much better chance of getting ideas and scripts accepted if you know how to edit your own tape – at least to a 'rough-cut' state. This chapter looks at technical developments which have affected broadcasting over the years, and then shows you how to edit audio-tape yourself.

Broadcasting was transformed by the invention of the portable tape recorder. Until the late 1940s the standard method of recording was on big slow-speed acetate discs. The heavy twin-tabled recording gear was mounted in large saloon cars from which the microphones would be run out on long cables. This cumbersome paraphernalia put severe limitations on where recordings could be made. It also meant that a recording team with its driver and engineer was nearly the size of a film crew, and recording sessions had to be planned carefully in advance.

Editing with slow-speed discs was a complex business. One of the best-known programmes to be recorded on location was Wilfred Pickles' quiz show, *Have a Go*. This took up several discs and did not always run to time, so a certain amount of cutting had to be done to fit the programme to its slot. The discs were recorded with an overlap, and on transmission the operator would start the two discs and get them running side by side in sync. for a few moments before mixing over from one to the next. It was possible sometimes to shorten the recording by lifting the needle early on disc one, or dropping it late on disc two. But Wilfred sometimes got carried away by his live audience, and either the backchat and repartee would become indiscreet or some competitor would mention a brand name or make a libellous statement which could not be broadcast. This would somehow have to be removed from the middle of a disc. If time permitted this could be done by 'dubbing off' (copying), but since the programme was often recorded only hours before transmission, time was at a premium and the editing had to be done by 'jump-cuts'. The discs would be marked up with chinagraph pencil, and as the operator played them on the air he would listen with a cue sheet, lift the needle at the critical point, and drop it again *on the right groove* a few seconds farther on. This called for nerve and skill, and I have often seen the operator emerge from the Manchester studio limp with exhaustion after a gruelling session of playing *Have a Go* with more than its usual quota of jump-cuts.

The advent of magnetic tape changed all this. Programmes could now be recorded and replayed continuously, whatever the duration, and any necessary cuts could easily be made with a razor-blade and a reel of splicing tape.

It took time to develop a truly portable recorder. The heavy and cumbersome 'Midget' recorder was scarcely worthy of the name, but it released the broadcaster from the umbilical cord of the recording car. He became free to make recordings wherever and whenever he chose, and the age of unscripted actuality was born.

Now that the tyranny of the script and the formal recording session had been broken the way was clear for a whole fresh class of broadcaster to take to the air. Men and women who fluffed and stumbled, who spoke in thick dialect and found it impossible to read fluently from a script, were 'discovered' as a new and exciting source of broadcast material. Even tapes recorded by someone with a pronounced stutter could be cleaned up to produce a smooth and apparently spontaneous result. There were times when the whole personality of a speaker was removed by over-enthusiastic editing, but the tape recorder was a big bonus for the radio producer.

The birth of the radio ballad

One man who saw the imaginative and creative possibilities in this new technology was Charles Parker, a BBC Producer in Birmingham. He started to collect recordings of men and women talking about their work and experiences of life, and was struck by the natural vitality of this sort of talk, and how impossible it was ever to re-create it in the studio with actors. He had the idea of telling a dramatic story entirely through words spoken by the actual people to whom it had happened, using no narrator, but only the authentic voices edited into a montage and heightened by music. He chose as collaborators the poet and folk singer Ewan McColl and the musician Peggy Seeger, and the result was a new art form — the radio ballad.

The first radio ballad told the story of John Axon, the driver of a runaway goods train who stayed on his footplate when he could have jumped to safety. He failed to regain control of his engine and was killed when he crashed into a train in front. *The Ballad of John Axon* was first broadcast in 1958, and was a sensation. John Axon was followed by a programme about the North Sea fishermen, *Singing the Fishing*, which won the Italia Prize. Here is how Charles Parker himself described the process of creating a radio ballad:

> You go out and talk for hours and hours and hours with the people who are the subject, not interviewing them, just listening to them, so that you begin to get under your belt as a writer, as a producer, as a singer, what it's like to be a fisherman, or to be a fisherman's wife, and to live in a fishing community; and you record also all the sounds that surround this activity as part of the scene in which this life takes place, and you come away — as we came away in this case — with something like fifty or sixty hours of material. You then transcribe that, and from those transcriptions you write songs, and you begin to see a pattern for a programme called, in this case, *Singing the Fishing*. It's called 'THE fishing', and that very simple use of the definite article carries a tremendous weight. Like 'Fisher' — when you say 'I'm fisher' that means 'fisher-folk', and much stronger than 'fisher-folk' it carries all sorts of undertones of struggle and hardship and privation and pride. That's what you learn when you listen.

Ewan McColl, Charles Parker's folk-singer/collaborator, had this advice for young people going into radio or television:

> I would say the first thing is to learn how to listen. And fortunately one has a machine which is a constant guide and a constant friend in helping one to learn how to listen and that machine is the tape recorder. I would say, go out, as we did...with a tape recorder and start off with the premise that you know nothing, but that out there in the big world outside there are people who know everything if you're prepared to listen. And if one is humble enough to...engage a bus driver or a waitress, or a building worker or whatever for as long as they're prepared to talk, then you will get something absolutely fantastic. At first people will tell you the things they think you want to hear, then they'll talk off the top of their heads. But there will come a time when they get tired of doing that and what will come out is something very very important and very very beautiful. . . .

Listening to *The Ballad of John Axon*, or to *Singing the Fishing* is a riveting experience. At the time of writing recordings are still available in libraries, and once in a while they are given the accolade of repeat broadcasts. Charles Parker died sadly young, but his work was a landmark in the recognition of the poetic value of vernacular speech. It is good to know that his tapes and materials have been collected together under the auspices of the Charles Parker Archive Trust, set up by his friends at Birmingham Public Library. Among dedicated radio-writers his name will not be forgotten.

Recording equipment

Today every other person owns a cassette tape recorder, often small and light enough to carry in a pocket. For the professional broadcaster, however, an open-reel machine is still essential. Audio tape runs at four standard speeds: 15, $7\frac{1}{2}$, $3\frac{3}{4}$ and $1\frac{7}{8}$ inches per second. The higher the tape speed the better the quality of recording and reproduction. Broadcasting companies tend to use 15 ips for music, in order to accommodate the full frequency range required. $7\frac{1}{2}$ ips produces acceptable quality for speech, and tapes recorded at this speed are easy to edit. It is possible, though more difficult, to razor-edit $3\frac{3}{4}$ ips tapes, but with the narrower cassette tapes recorded at $1\frac{7}{8}$ ips the only option is to edit electronically by dubbing (copying). If you have valuable material on a cassette tape, however, it is possible to copy it up onto open reel tape at a higher speed and edit it in that form.

It is never satisfactory to rely on the integral microphone supplied with many cassette-recorders, except for the most basic purposes – for example to tape the speeches at a meeting for subsequent transcription. The best possible microphone is always an investment, and it should be fitted with sufficient length of cable to enable you to set it up well away from the actual recording machine, in order to avoid picking up motor noise.

If you plan to do a lot of broadcasting you will need a stop-watch as well. Make sure you buy the type that will accumulate – i.e. one that you will be able to stop and re-start without re-setting. You can then time the cuts in a talk or recording as you make them, without constantly having to re-time the whole thing from the beginning.

Most modern tape recorders are half-track, i.e. you can make a first recording with the tape running one way and then turn the reel over and make a second recording on the other half of the tape, running in the reverse direction. Don't be tempted to do this if there is any likelihood that you will ever wish to edit the tape. It is a false economy. As soon as you cut one track you will also automatically cut the other.

There are several mains-operated machines on the market capable of recording at three of the four standard speeds, but if you need the freedom of a battery-operated recorder that will provide broadcast quality the field is more limited. For many years the standard tool of the radio reporter has been the UHER, which runs either on mains electricity or re-chargeable batteries. This piece of essential professional equipment will set you back more than £800. Some radio stations will lend UHERs to freelance contributors who know how to use them. There is talk of a new portable battery/mains tape recorder coming onto the market, but whatever the machine you record with, although it may improve the technical quality of your recording, it will not alter the value of what you put on the tape.

Editing audio-tape

The technique of razor-editing is simple. You need:

   a white or yellow chinagraph pencil
   a one-sided razor-blade or surgical scalpel
   a reel of special splicing tape
   reels of coloured leader tape – red, green and white
   an EMI editing block

The EMI editing block is a solid block of metal measuring about 6 inches long by 1 inch wide by $\frac{1}{2}$ inch deep, with a quarter inch channel down the middle, intersected by three narrow grooves running at 90, 45 and 33 degrees to the central channel. I have only ever used the 45 degree groove. Do not be tempted into buying smaller light-weight blocks, or gadgets with springs and grips for holding the tape – they are more trouble than they are worth.

The technique is as follows:

1) Mark the tape with the chinagraph pencil either side of the desired cut. In order to do this it is often necessary to unscrew the cover of the tape recorder to gain access to the replay head. Put the machine into *play* mode and activate the *pause* control. You should then be able to rotate the tape-reels by hand very slowly so as to identify the exact point at which a word or a cough begins or ends. This is called 'rock and roll' editing.

2) Lay the tape in the central channel so that the first mark falls on the 45 degree cross-groove, and cut it with the scalpel. Leave the end of tape you want to keep lying in the channel.

3) Bring up the other end of the tape, lay the mark on the groove, and cut it with the scalpel. You can now lift away the excised section of tape, leaving the two bits you want to keep held end-to-end in the central channel. (Don't throw away the discarded section yet.)

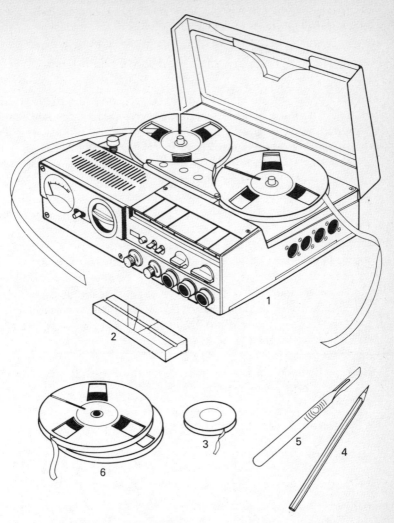

Key: 1 Tape recorder
      2 EMI block
      3 Splicing tape
      4 Chinagraph pencil
      5 Scalpel
      6 Red & green leader tape

4) Cut a $\frac{1}{2}$-inch bit of splicing tape and lay it over the join, pressing it well down to make sure it sticks.

5) Remove your edited tape from the block and check the edit by running it through the tape-recorder and listening to it critically.

You may change your mind about the way you have cut the tape, and it is perfectly possible to stick a section of excised tape back and re-edit at a different point, *provided you have kept the bit you cut and remember which way the tape runs*. I have always found it a useful practice to hang the surplus tape round my neck until I have checked the edit.

Put a length of green leader-tape at the start of your edited tape, and a length of red at the end. Intermediate sections can, if you like, be marked with white leader. Make sure your leaders are long enough to go round the tape decks of the large professional machines in a broadcasting studio.

Editing is time-consuming and tedious, but the more practice you have the faster you can get. It is valuable to be able to do it on your own at home instead of having to book expensive studio sessions.

Although it is legitimate to remove long pauses in a recording of a hesitant speaker, it is important to retain the natural gaps between words and phrases. For this reason, when marking the tape, make the first mark at the start of the first word to be cut, and the second mark at the start of the first word to be heard after the cut, thus retaining the natural pacing of the sentence. For example:

'... sounds that surround this activity as part of the − /part of the sort of − /scene in which this life takes place'

Not

'... sounds that surround this activity as part of the/ − part of the sort of − /scene in which this life takes place'

In the hands of an unscrupulous editor a tape can be made to suggest that a speaker said things he did not say. Negatives can be removed, words transposed, whole sentences built up from different sections of the original tape, and when replayed the cuts will be undetectable. In the hands of a Goebbels audio tape could be a devastating weapon of propaganda. Fortunately, in Britain traditions of integrity in radio journalism ensure that tape editing is used with discretion to enhance the acceptability of a speaker and not to distort his views.

Recording conditions

The quality of recorded sound is affected by the surroundings in which the recording is made. Large echoing rooms with hard shiny surfaces such as polished floors and plate glass windows tend to give unsatisfactory results. Try to find a small room or the corner of a corridor. Draw curtains across windows, and put a blanket or coat on a table under the microphone to deaden reflections.

Listen for intrusive external noises such as lawn-mowers or vacuum cleaners, and try to get them halted while you are recording. If an aircraft flies overhead, stop your recording and restart after it has passed. Not only will irrelevant sounds be a distraction, they will make it difficult for you to edit the tape. If Concorde flying overhead suddenly stops dead because you cut out the next sentence your listeners will wonder what has happened.

Music in the background adds another hazard – that of copyright. If you are not able to provide full details of composer, performers and recording label of any music heard on your tape it may be impossible to clear copyright, and consequently impossible to broadcast it. A cautionary example is the song *Happy birthday to you*. This is in copyright, and a fee is payable every time it is broadcast.

There is no doubt that the skilful inclusion of appropriate background sounds can create an atmosphere of authenticity in a broadcast, and give the listener a sense of actually being there. It is difficult, however, to judge the balance of these against voices when you are recording. The wisest course is to make two separate recordings, one in a quiet corner carrying your interview or whatever, and one carrying the sound effects which can eventually be mixed in at the right level in the studio when the tapes are broadcast.

Before you set out to make a recording involving anyone else, make sure you are perfectly familiar with your equipment, and make a test recording before you start. Don't forget to de-activate the replay volume, otherwise you will get a 'howl-round' the minute you open the microphone. If the tape doesn't move when you switch on, this is probably because it has been incorrectly laced, or you have depressed the pause control and forgotten to release it.

Rewind your tapes, box them and label them carefully with date, contents, and speed of recording. A surprising amount of time can be wasted discovering that tapes are back to front, or don't carry the material you thought they did.

Good luck and good hunting!

4
Drama on the Air

Every afternoon – and several time a week in the evening – the BBC broadcasts a radio play in its domestic services. The World Service also has its own drama department. Many BBC plays reach still wider audiences through the Transcription Service, or the sale of recordings to the public. The result is that far more people listen to a radio play than could possibly attend a theatre during a run in London's West End. No wonder many famous writers have thought it worth while to write for this enormous and far-flung audience, and many writers now distinguished in other media, including film and television, served an initial apprenticeship in this fascinating and demanding field.

Although radio drama is a good deal cheaper to produce than television it is more costly than other forms of programming, and radio networks financed by advertising find commercial pressures towards inexpensive mass-appeal pop-music/chat-show formats almost irresistible. Across the Atlantic radio plays have virtually disappeared from the air waves. Nevertheless, some Independent Local Radio stations in Britain continue to keep the drama flag flying. In 1987 the IBA entered a play from Radio Clyde for the prestigious international Italia Prize contest, and LBC are broadcasting, in a series of five-minute instalments, an adaptation of *Pepys' Diary*, which has been made for them by Independent Radio Drama Productions Ltd. Other local radio stations have transmitted plays written by listeners in their reception area, or productions made by local schoolchildren in association with Educational Producers.

Dramatic structure

What makes a good radio play? To answer that question we must first consider what makes a good play in any medium, and then look at factors which lend themselves especially to radio presentation. The classic elements without which effective drama cannot exist are: an initial conflict, mounting tension, a climax, and a resolution.

Plays are made up of a sequence of scenes, which can be considered as the foothills of a mountain. As the foothills rise and fall, each one getting higher than the last until the summit is reached, so should each scene be a microcosm of the whole, with its own internal tension, climax and resolution. Although the first draft of a play, dashed off in the white heat of inspiration, may not conform to these requirements, careful editing with this structure in mind will undoubtedly heighten its dramatic effect.

Theme and plot

As well as this basic structure, our play will have a plot, characters and a theme. The plot is the sequence of events which take place in the action, the characters are the people to whom they happen, and the theme underlying the whole thing is what the play is really about. Let us suppose our play tells the story of a man climbing a mountain. The plot is constructed so as to give him various difficulties and hazards to overcome, and brings him into contact with other characters who interact with him. But the same story can be used to illustrate a number of different themes – the struggle of man against nature, self-discovery through confrontation with danger, the indomitability of the human spirit, the nature of ambition, and so on. The theme is the true *raison d'être* of the play, an internal pulse which beats like a heart throughout the action and gives it significance.

Pros and cons of the medium

Now let us consider the limitations imposed by the medium of radio, and the freedoms which it bestows. First, and most obvious, the audience cannot see.

Richard Hughes, the writer of the very first radio play, *Danger*, broadcast in 1924, turned this to good account by placing his characters in the same position as his audience – he set his story in a coal-mine. The first words are 'What's happened?' 'The lights have gone out.' Immediately listeners can identify with the small group caught in the nightmare of a pit accident, underground in the dark.

The radio writer cannot call on the resources of scenery, lighting and costume to reinforce his message. The silent visual *coup de théâtre* is denied him. He uses words, together with any appropriate sound effects, to create atmosphere in the mind of the listener. For this is the theatre of the mind, wherein the writer can move his characters instantly backwards through the centuries or forwards into the future. He can set the first scene on an airliner and the next at the bottom of the sea. If he chooses to send his protagonist to the South Pole we can go with him every step of the way. This is liberation indeed.

What is more, although the characters in a radio play must use human language they don't have to be human beings. Animals, plants and inanimate objects can be brought to articulate life and pressed into service as part of the cast. Radio lends itself particularly well to fantasy, witness the much-loved *Toy-town* and *Wind in the Willows*, and Douglas Adams' cult success, *Hitch-hiker's Guide to the Galaxy*.

This aspect of radio was brilliantly exploited by J.C.W. Brook in his play, *Giving Up*. The theme is one man's efforts to give up smoking. The cast list features all the parts of the body, including ears, nose, mouth, arms, legs, fingers, private parts, brain, will, conscience and so on. This is how the play opens:

	SLEEP NOISES FROM ALL OVER THE BODY.
RIGHT EAR	Right Ear to Brain, Right Ear to Brain . . .
LEFT EAR	(OVERLAPS) Left Ear to Brain, Left Ear to Brain . . .
RIGHT EAR	You keep out of this. I heard it first.
LEFT EAR	I'm only doing my job. When I hear something I report it. Left Ear to Brain, Left Ear to Brain . . .
RIGHT EAR	(OVERLAPS) Right Ear to Brain, Right Ear to Brain. GRUNTS AND GROANS AND BESTIRRING NOISES FROM ALL OVER THE BODY.
OMNES	Shut up Ears . . . Go back to sleep . . . Stuff some cotton wool in your orifices . . . etc.
BRAIN	(WAKES) Errrmmmm . . . ahhh . . . ummm?
EARS	Alarm Clock, Brain – alarm clock; time to get up. RINGING OF ALARM CLOCK COMES ECHOING THROUGH EARS.
BRAIN	Oh dear . . .
RIGHT ARM	Right Arm here, Brain. The usual?
BRAIN	Ummm, please.
RIGHT ARM	Stretching now . . . (STRETCHING NOISES) O.K. Fingers, first one on the button gets a manicure.

Giving Up, J.C.W. Brook (BBC Playscripts)

And so the play continues with dialogue between all the different elements that make up a man, and increasing conflict between his Brain, his Will, and his Conscience. It's extremely ingenious, highly effective radio, and would be hard to realise in any other medium.

Dialogue and characterisation

Now for the nitty-gritty of a radio play – the dialogue. In radio the dialogue has to do much more than in any other dramatic medium. It has to carry the plot forward, portray the characters, place them in time and space, provide the props and paint the scenery. It has, too, to convey every human emotion – joy and despair, comedy and tragedy.

In these multifarious tasks it can be supported by music and effects, but music and effects cannot relieve the dialogue of its responsibilities – they can only assist it.

Each character should have an aurally recognisable personality. Some of this can be achieved in production by clever casting, but the groundwork must be laid by the playwright. A scene which calls for an argument between four middle-class middle-aged women will have to be skilfully acted indeed for the listener to be able to tell who is saying what. By creating scenes in which, to take crude examples, man talks to woman, foreigner to Englishman, child to adult, and not allowing too many people to join in at once, the writer automatically makes it easier for the listener to keep his bearings and differentiate between the characters.

Make sure that the characters talk consistently all the way through. A useful exercise is to read aloud all the lines given to one character, end to end in sequence throughout a play, leaving out the speeches in between. This will often throw up lines which are patently out of character, and indicate places where characterisation can be strengthened.

Although, as we have seen, radio is an intimate medium, it is not enough for dialogue to mimic the diffuse exchanges of normal conversation. Dramatically effective dialogue is everyday speech boiled-down into a concentrated essence, in which every word has a reason for being there, whether to illustrate character, to carry the plot forward, or to build atmosphere and a sense of location. Do not overlook the potential of monologue. Shakespeare's soliloquies take on new power and significance when we hear them spoken softly as if we are in truth eavesdropping on Hamlet's thoughts, rather than having them belted out across the footlights in order to reach the farthest corner of the gallery. There have been highly successful radio plays for one voice only.

Strong language

A word about strong language. There are many members of the radio audience who are deeply offended by swearing, blasphemy and the use of four-letter Anglo-Saxon words for functions of the body. This makes it difficult for the writer to provide convincing dialogue for characters whose everyday speech draws freely on such resources. A glance at Bob Geldof's autobiography will illustrate this amply. The fact remains that strong language is unacceptable as normal currency on the air. It is perfectly possible to create scenes of obscenity and sexual violence without using a single offensive word, and it is a test of writing skill to do this. In the end, the frequent use of bad language only weakens its effect.

The deliberate choice of a single shocking word at a climactic point may be dramatically essential. The classic example is Bernard Shaw in *Pygmalion*, when he makes Eliza Doolittle ejaculate 'Not bloody likely' in the middle of a polite tea-party. She would have to use a stronger word than 'bloody' to produce a comparable effect today, but the principle is the same.

Dialect

Characters who speak in dialect can be useful as a contrast to other voices (provided the whole play is not in dialect!), but beware of spelling out phonetically the lines given to such characters. The writer should make use of the idioms and turns of phrase natural to the dialect in question, and indicate in the list of characters that this person is a Scot or a Geordie, or whatever. The Producer will cast a player who is good at this particular accent, and he will do the rest. Actors find phonetic spelling at best irritating, and at worst a real hindrance to interpretation. They also prefer not to have words underlined to indicate stress. Sentences should be written so that the intended meaning is clear without underscoring particular words. Different interpretations can develop and emphases can change in a remarkable way in the course of rehearsal.

Moving characters in time and space

Now to locating the action. In a radio play there is no printed programme in which you can brief the audience 'Scene 1: Bert's living room. . . . Scene 2: Next morning at the boat house' etc. The locations and the passage of time must be indicated through the dialogue. A useful convention has grown up in the use of fades. A fade-out followed by a fade-up is clearly understood by the audience to signal a lapse of time and/or a change of location. These developments must, however, be 'signposted' in the dialogue. For example:

BERT   Right, then, I'll meet you at the boat-house tomorrow
            morning. 6.30, and don't oversleep, you old
            slug-a-bed.
TOM   (MOVING OFF) I'll be there, never fear.
BERT   (CALLING AFTER HIM) Make sure you are, then!
            (FADE)
            FADE UP OPEN AIR ACOUSTIC. NOISE OF
            LAPPING WATER.

BERT   Ah! Tom! You made it! Wonders will never cease.
TOM   (APPROACHING, YAWNING) I don't deny it was
          an effort. I say, the river's high this morning. . . .

Note that we did not have to hear a door open and shut at the end of the first scene as Tom left, and we certainly don't need footsteps. Footsteps are hardly ever necessary, and when they are required to make a special impact (for example, echoing in a passageway as the villain stalks the heroine at dead of night in a thriller) it is often difficult to make them sound convincing. They have to be made on the correct surface, in the right perspective with the actors' voices, and they need literally to be acted out in the studio. Although recorded footsteps may be available they seldom ring true, and an immense amount of rehearsal time can be taken up getting footsteps just right. Don't call for them in your script unless they are absolutely essential.

Effects, perspective and acoustic

Sound effects (often written FX in a script) should be used with discretion to create atmosphere rather than as a primary vehicle of information. The best effects are clear precise noises which are easily recognisable. The much-maligned BBC seagull is a good example. A ship's hooter, a cuckoo, the cooing of doves, the call of an owl, a grandfather clock striking – all these convey instant atmosphere. Mushy sounds such as traffic, rain and crackling fires are not immediately identifiable for what they are, and are much less effective.

A surprising amount of information can be conveyed by the use of perspective and acoustic. Entrances and exits are achieved by getting a character to approach or move away from the microphone, and good radio actors are very skilled in this technique. Voices in a small room sound quite different from voices in the echoing spaces of a cathedral or in the deadness of the open air, and the listener is sensitive to these distinctions. Drama studios are equipped to provide a range of acoustics. Through the control panel different degrees of artificial echo can be added to make variations between one scene and the next, and there may well be an 'an-echoic' chamber where actors can play scenes set out of doors. For this reason you should include in your script clear indications of the location of each scene, even though you don't need to give a visual description.

The advent of stereophonic recording has made it possible to give highly realistic aural pictures of the action in a play, in which characters can be heard moving about almost as if they were on stage in a theatre. To get the full stereo effect, however, the listener must place himself accurately in relation to the loudspeakers or else listen on headphones.

Most of the audience will not be doing this, and reception on the average domestic receiver falls far short of the exacting standards in a broadcasting studio. The writer must therefore not depend on skilful stereo reproduction to convey information. The play must 'work' and be fully understandable at a much less sophisticated technical level.

The listener remains with the microphone, wherever you decide to put it, and to take the microphone for a walk with two characters while they talk to each other is seldom effective. There will be no sense of movement, even if (perish the thought!) you add footsteps. It will be better to start your two characters off on their walk by fading them out as they move into the distance, and then leap-frog the microphone ahead of them, so that you hear them approaching. You can do this several times, and it works well. Note that there is a difference between a move off and a fade-out. The first indicates a simple exit, while the second suggests a lapse of time as well.

Some years ago the actor-manager Timothy West wrote a short play called *This Gun that I Have in My Right Hand is Loaded*. This hilarious piece neatly sends up the conventions of radio drama. The fact is that although the conventions work they have to be used with subtlety and discretion. I am grateful to Mr West for permission to include his masterpiece at the end of this book, as a cautionary example for aspiring radio playwrights.

Music

Music is a powerful generator of atmosphere and mood, and can be introduced in several ways. Perhaps one of the characters is a musician, and the music he plays is an integral part of the action. Or perhaps a particular passage is used to signal, say, the appearance of a ghost, or the revival of a memory. Or the music may simply give the listener a clue as to the sort of story he is going to be offered, romantic or humorous, sinister or gay.

The selection of music is part of the Producer's job, but the writer can make suggestions if he wishes. It is often difficult to find passages of the right length and scale in standard musical works, and electronic music may be the most appropriate choice. In the early 1950s a small group of studio engineers and music balancers at the BBC began to experiment with the manufacture of all sorts of unusual sounds, musical and otherwise, and their efforts led to the establishment of the BBC Radiophonic Workshop. This is a department which employs composers and electronic engineers, and radio and TV Producers can now commission it to supply suitable music and effects for radio or television productions of all sorts, ranging from comedy shows such as the *Goons*, through a whole gamut of signature tunes for regular programmes, to prestige wild-life spectaculars.

A spin-off from this development is that the BBC now possesses an extensive library of specially composed electronic music and sounds on which it can draw for current productions, without incurring the copyright fees inevitably attracted by the use of commercial recordings.

Titles and synopses

Let us suppose that an idea for a radio play has hatched in your fertile mind. You have been mulling over the plot and its underlying theme for some time, and now you can hear the characters beginning to talk. Think of a title, even if it is only a temporary working title. This often helps to clarify the theme. Write a synopsis, a bare outline of the plot, on a single page. Draw up a list of the main characters and give them names. There is a need for a lot more information about them than will actually be given in the script. Your play will take place at a climactic point in their lives, and you need to know them so thoroughly that you can imagine how they will behave and talk under any circumstances. The situations in which you place them will create the drama.

As you proceed with the actual writing you will find yourself referring back to the synopsis and character sketches that you prepared to start with. You may want to modify them as the play takes on a life of its own, but your original notes will help you to be consistent, and to produce something with a strong basic structure.

The BBC Radio Drama Script Unit produces a useful leaflet which will show you, among other things, how to set the script out on the page. The most important thing is to make a clear distinction between words meant to be spoken as dialogue and instructions as to sound effects and stage directions. Allow wide margins, double spacing between each speech, and use only one side of the paper.

The right ending

Bear in mind that a play should be conceived not merely as a tale that is told; this is the province of the short story or the novel. A play should be an experience shared between the characters and the audience. The listener must live through the events portrayed and participate in the emotions and motivations of those to whom they happen. He must be able to identify himself with at least one of these characters, and feel concern and involvement in the outcome of the events. At the end, we must be left with a sense of 'rightness'. Whether the conclusion is happy or sad, the audience must not feel cheated. The ending should tidy up any unfinished business left hanging in the plot and return us to the level of everyday life from the heightened tensions of dramatic experience.

Perhaps one could parallel the mental experience of listening to a play with the physical experience of a searching physical work-out, ending with a short period of relaxation, and leaving behind a sensation of adjustment, balance, and well-being. Maybe this is what Aristotle had in mind when he wrote of 'catharsis'. Jean-Louis Barrault puts it like this:

> In fact, at the theatre, we are always assisting at a vast settling of accounts. From all the opposing rights, from the Rugby scrum of rights, there should by degrees emerge a Sentence. Justice. And the spectator isn't satisfied unless the sentence is just. Just, not in relation to the individuals participating in the conflict, but in relation to Life, in the universal sense of the word ... Always make sure that the universal spirit of justice has been respected in a play. If not: beware of the mood of the audience.
>
> From *Reflections on the Theatre*, Jean-Louis Barrault (Rockliff 1951)

Here is the check-list which readers for the BBC Radio Drama Script Unit are asked to apply, before recommending a play for production:

1) Why did you enjoy it?
2) Was it a good story?
3) Are the characters as good as the story?
4) Does it make good use of the medium of radio?
5) Is the beginning good enough?

5
Serials and Soap-Operas: Writing in a Team

There is a difference between a serial play and a soap opera. A serial play is complete in itself, although it may be broken up into several instalments. It may be an original story, or the dramatisation of a novel, but it will have a beginning, a middle and an end. A soap opera, on the other hand, is a continuously unfolding saga about a group of characters and their daily lives. It may go on for years, and when it starts no-one can foresee what the end will be – if, in fact, it ever has one. The term 'soap opera' for this form of drama is said to have originated in the USA, because it was so popular as a means of promoting the sales of soap powders. A serial play will probably be scripted by one writer, while a soap opera will involve a team. Famous serials have included Galsworthy's *The Forsyte Saga*, novels by Jane Austen and Trollope, and more recently Tolkien's *The Lord of the Rings*.

Probably the best-known soap opera in the world is *The Archers*, which has been running on BBC six days a week since 1951. This 'everyday story of country folk' was conceived by Godfrey Baseley, at that time the BBC's farming talks producer in the Midlands. He wanted to devise a programme to which farmers and their families would enjoy listening, and at the same time absorb a certain amount of accurate information about current thinking in the agricultural world. With the years the emphasis has shifted from information to entertainment, but the programme still has an agricultural adviser and is as true to present-day farming life as possible. When it was launched no-one dreamed how popular it would become. Nowadays, as well as two daily UK transmissions Monday to Friday and an omnibus edition on Sundays, *The Archers* goes to many overseas destinations, courtesy of the BBC Transcription Service. Recordings are made available to the British Forces Broadcasting Service a fortnight ahead of transmission, so that service families on foreign stations can listen to the programmes on the same day as those at home in Britain, and so keep in touch with the changing seasons and day-to-day concerns of an English village community. *The Archers* has not been the only British radio serial. There was the adventure serial, *Dick Barton, Special Agent*, the domestic *Mrs Dale's Diary*, and others. Now the BBC has launched *Citizens* on Radio 4, so the form is still very much alive.

Schedules

Writing scripts for a serial means contributing to a tightly co-ordinated operation. Getting a daily instalment on the air calls for a production-line approach which is somewhat different from the way in which many creative writers like to work. Scripts must be the right length, well-plotted and researched, skilfully characterised, written within a specified time-span, and delivered to a deadline. A late script, or one that needs re-writing, will hold up the whole conveyor-belt. It is not practical to keep a daily serial on the air with only one writer, although this can be done for short periods. The normal practice is to have a team of writers, who are given a week's episodes at a time to write. *The Archers* is run on a four-week cycle, and the following dates from the summer of 1987 are given as an example:

Tuesday July 14th: All day script meeting with four writers, Editor, Producer, Programme Assistant, Agricultural Adviser and probably others. The programme has a number of advisers — Medical, Church, Land Agency, and so on — and any of them may be at the script meeting. Four weeks' scripts are discussed and the main plot-lines agreed. Writers divided into two pairs, A and B.

Tuesday July 21st: Pair A writers telephone in their cast requirements, and follow this up as quickly as possible with synopses of their episodes.

Monday July 27th: Pair B writers do the same.

Tuesday July 28th: Pair A deliver their scripts (5 each).

Tuesday August 4th: Pair B deliver their scripts (5 each).

Wednesday/Thursday/Friday August 19th–21st: Pair A scripts recorded (10 instalments in 3 days).

Wednesday/Thursday/Friday August 26th–28th: Pair B scripts recorded (10 instalments in 3 days).

Weeks beginning 7th and 14th September: Pair A scripts transmitted.

Weeks beginning 21st and 28th September: Pair B scripts transmitted.

You will see that, if you are chosen as the first writer of Pair A, you will have exactly fourteen days in which to write and deliver your five scripts. They will be recorded four weeks later, and transmitted two weeks after that.

The schedule for *Citizens* is slightly different. As there are to be three broadcasts each week (two 25-minute instalments plus an omnibus edition on Saturdays) a team of three writers has been assembled, and the production timetable drawn up on a three-weekly basis. The cycle starts with a Tuesday script meeting, after which each writer turns in a synopsis for one week's scripts by the following Friday. Fourteen days after the script meeting all three writers deliver their scripts, and these are recorded fourteen days later.

In the gap between script meeting and recording all sorts of things may go wrong. A plot line one writer wants to emphasise may not have been set up sufficiently by the preceding writer. An actor may have taken work elsewhere and become unavailable for recording. Another actor playing a key character may be taken ill, and an episode have to be re-written. Some event may occur in the real world which cannot be ignored in a programme with any pretensions to topicality. This sort of emergency can be handled provided the system works, and any unnecessary crises are avoided. Getting efficient scripts in on time is a key element of the system.

Plotting

Writers receive copies of all the latest story lines and are asked how they think these plots should be developed. They are also asked to come up with new ideas of their own. They should bring all this to the script meeting and take part in the discussion, which is the most creative part of the 'soap-making' process. The story lines grow out of the discussion, and writers pool their ideas at the script meeting. They sometimes have to accept that someone else is going to be given the chance to write their bright invention – all part of the angst of being a team member.

If you become part of this operation you will have to take acount of the story up to the point at which you take over, and what you write will affect what everyone else writes afterwards. You will be presented with the main set of characters on whom you can draw, each of them with a fully developed life history, likes, dislikes and ways of behaviour. All sorts of things are 'known' about these people, from long before they ever appeared in the serial, and you will have to familiarise yourself with them, their backgrounds, and the geography of their surroundings. Actors are booked *ad hoc*, and the production office will have to make sure which of the regular performers are available before you write those characters into your script. Extra characters you may wish to bring in will be rationed. It's important to have mercy on the writer who will follow you, and not to leave him to pick up an under-developed plot line, or to extricate the characters

from an impossible predicament. Think your situations right through –
it isn't always practical to use the old Dick Barton get-out 'With one
bound he was free!'

Structure

Each episode of *The Archers* lasts fifteen minutes, which means in
practice a reading-out-loud time of about thirteen minutes. Each
instalment usually contains five scenes, and not more than seven
characters. The plotting is the longest and most demanding part of the
process. Some writers actually do this on graph paper, ensuring that
storylines peak in the right places in the week to keep listeners tuned
in. Each writer should have been given a mix of plot-lines at the
meeting – something funny, something romantic, something agricultural etc. Each should get a clear idea of what his main story is for the
week, and his second story, and so on, otherwise the scripts can come
in flat. What the Producer looks for is peaks and troughs in the right
places.

Each 15-minute episode needs to be planned for a good mix. A
writer should ask himself if there is a variety of tones. An echo-y barn
interior might follow a breezy scene on Lakey Hill; a cosy slow-
moving chat among the old folk of Ambridge might be followed by a
snappy, funny scene with younger characters; an emotional scene
might need a comic scene to pick the audience up again. Each scene
need to 'thicken' at its ending, and in some way signpost the listeners
on: the momentum of a soap is always onwards. There might be three
peaks in a week as the different storylines come to fruition, and the last
scene on a Friday needs a good strong ending. It can just be a happy
ending, or a mysterious one, or a funny one, but it certainly needs to be
strong.

Structuring scripts is the hardest and longest part of the process.
Writers send their synopses in before casting, and the Producer and
Editor hope to spot the structural errors before they go down on paper.
But telling a writer one scene doesn't work can bring his whole plan for
the week crumbling down around him, so writers need to be flexible.
The most common problem is the balancing of action and reaction.
How much should actually happen in a scene, and how much can be
reported action, or characterisation, or atmosphere? A useful guide-line
is that at least one piece of action should happen in every scene. It may
take place in the course of the dialogue (e.g. someone finds out
something they didn't know before), but there should be just one piece
of plot advancement. That leaves plenty of room for characterisation
etc., but it means the listeners who just want plot are getting a helping
in every scene.

The Archers has its own atmosphere. It reflects the tempo of life in a small rural community. If you were writing an adventure serial the pace would be much faster. There might well be three main peaks in each instalment. The first few minutes would deal with the situation obtaining at the end of the previous transmission, and build up quickly to its conclusion. The tension could then be allowed to relax as a fresh situation was introduced and developed. This in its turn would be tidied up, in time to present the third situation, which as it unfolded would generate more tension, culminating in a peak of excitement at the end of the instalment. This situation would be resolved at the start of the next day's broadcast. And so on. The most important peak – in the case of an adventure serial this would be a genuine cliff-hanger – would come at the end of the week's episodes, to hook the audience firmly into switching on again next week.

Citizens is neither an adventure serial nor a country yarn, but set among young people making their way in life, so the atmosphere will be different again. Five men and women who first met as students come together to share a crumbling house in a London suburb. They are drawn from four very different families, and the serial focuses on these main characters and follows them into their working lives, and from time to time back to the families around the United Kingdom.

The 'landlady' of the house shared by the five is Alex Parker. She is the mother of Baby William, and has a job at Bread Street Arts Centre. There is a doctor in the house, a Hindu from Birmingham, called Anita Sharma. Julia Brennan and her twin brother Mike are from an Irish Catholic family in Liverpool; Julia is a trainee manager at a London department store, and Mike is unemployed and drifting. The fifth resident is Hugh Hamilton from Kilmarnock in Scotland, who has a job with a prestigious merchant bank. At the time of writing the first episode has not yet been broadcast, and it will be interesting to see how the characters develop from this initial plan.

Openings

If you feel brave enough to risk your sanity on the treadmill of serial-writing, start by listening regularly, so that you absorb the atmosphere and characters of the main protagonists, and know instinctively how they would talk and react to different situations. Then write to the Producer and say you would like to try your hand. You will probably be sent a 'Writer's Pack' with all the key information, and invited to submit a trial script, either the next one after a current episode, or a completely independent one of your own devising, using main characters but ignoring current plot lines.

Liz Rigbey, Producer of *The Archers*, says 'I'm looking for writers who know the programme, something of its history, and who are familiar with our characters. We decide what is to happen in Ambridge at our monthly script meetings and it's essential to me to have writers who can play a useful part at this stage of the process, i.e. who are prepared to come up with ideas and aren't too shy to deliver them. Finally, it's no good coming to *The Archers* if you're going to get miffed when the script editor does her job. First time around, we'd expect to rework at least 30 per cent of a writer's scripts. Sometimes we hardly have to change a word; sometimes they have to be completely rewritten. If, after a commission, someone delivers 75 minutes of promising material on time, if we've enjoyed working with them and if their contribution to the script meeting was helpful, the chances are I'll offer them the chance to write another six weeks for us. Overall, it's fast and draining writing. Any writer on soap should make sure they're doing other stuff as well, to refresh them, and I won't let anyone write more than six weeks broadcasts a year for this reason. I'm not in the business of burning anyone out.'

So there it is – go to it, you gluttons for punishment!

6
Features and Documentaries

Asa Briggs, the historian of British broadcasting, considers the pioneering development of the radio feature one of the BBC's greatest contributions to the art of radio. Until the 1950s BBC Radio had a separate features department, under the guidance of Laurence Gilliam, who gathered under his wing a band of the most distinguished radio writers of the day. Legendary names such as D.G. Bridson, Louis MacNeice, Leonard Cottrell, Alan Burgess and W.R. Rodgers made the radio feature their own. Today Features are a sub-division of Drama Department, but the contribution of this section to the BBC output is outstanding in its originality and imaginative quality. Documentary techniques are used in other departments, of course, to present a wide range of material.

What is a feature? It is hard to arrive at a definition, for a wide range of subjects and treatments can shelter under this umbrella, bordering on drama on the one side and illustrated talks on the other. The one clear distinction between features and plays seems to be that features deal with fact while plays deal with fiction. A play may dramatise a true story, but by the invention of imaginary dialogue and perhaps by juggling with the time-scale of real events for dramatic purposes, the writer creates a fictitious product. The feature writer, on the other hand, while he may employ many ingenious and original techniques of presentation, will be scrupulous to include in his script only material for which he has firm evidence, and he must tell the story as it happened, eschewing the liberties of dramatic licence.

There is a category of programme lying between fiction and documentary which has come to be known as 'faction'. This is a sort of bastard form in which an account of true events is presented in a pseudo-documentary style, heightened by the inclusion of passages of imaginary dialogue. The listener does not know who is talking or on what authority, and by the end cannot tell how much of what he has heard is fact and how much fiction. I have a distaste for this category, and would urge radio writers to be rigorous in their rejection of it. Write a play, or write a feature, but don't confuse the two.

The list of titles given below, which is drawn at random from

Radio 4 billings over the past five or six years, will give some idea of the range of subjects dealt with in feature programmes:

Pandora's Box: a critical look at BBC journalism by Robert Carvel.

Malibran: a portrait of the famous nineteenth-century Spanish soprano by Peggy Branford.

The Bitter and the Sweet: the story of two pioneering sisters and their very different attitudes to life in the backwoods of Canada. Compiled and introduced by Margaret Horsfield.

Echoes of the Great War: based on the diary of over three million words kept by Andrew Clark, Rector of Great Leighs in Essex, by James Munson.

Up, You Mighty Race: Ferdy Dennis tells the story of Marcus Garvey, an almost forgotten Jamaican hero.

Shakespeare on his Lips: Simon Callow on Charles Laughton in the theatre.

Father of Fibre: The story of Surgeon-Captain T.L. Cleave, compiled, written and introduced by Adrian Mourby.

The techniques employed range from writers doing their own narration, with extracts from diaries and memoirs read by actors, through compilations of unscripted recordings, to full-scale dramatisations.

The role of the narrator

Because he is bound by the limitations of his documentation the features writer often finds himself in need of a narrator. A linking voice can be used in a number of different ways. Narration may be written in an impersonal style to be read by an actor or professional presenter with the sort of neutral delivery that will not obtrude a personality into the programme. This sort of narrative provides a detached and authoritative commentary – the voice of the broadcasting station, as it were. A development of this is to use two alternating narrators with contrasting voices, a man and a woman perhaps. This can be a useful device for leavening long passages of factual exposition.

If the writer is himself the broadcaster he can couch the narration in the first person. This frees him to express his own personal opinions, provided this is made clear to the listener. You can approach the task of writing narration for yourself to speak in the same way as you would tackle writing a talk. A script which calls for only a limited use of other voices may be classed as an illustrated talk, and this can have implications for your contract and fee. See Chapter 12.

A third possibility is to put linking narrative into the mouth of one of the main characters in the programme. This can be very effective if suitable contemporary material is available in the form of a diary or letters. Letters, indeed, have formed the basis of many successful radio scripts, both documentary features and plays.

Duration

The preferred duration for full-scale features seems to be about forty-five minutes, but depending on the nature of the material and the time slot they may be longer or shorter. Many magazine programmes regularly include 'featurettes', short reports lasting up to ten minutes, which usually consist of a compilation of unscripted interviews linked by narration. In collecting recordings for such reports the writer may wish to keep his own voice out of the programme. If he conducts the interviews skilfully it will be possible to edit out his questions, so that the results appear to be fluent statements by the interviewees. More guidance on interviewing techniques will be found in Chapter 8 on news and current affairs.

Anthologies, abridgements and adaptations

Under the heading 'features' we should also consider anthologies, abridgements and adaptations of existing works. There is an endless fund of themes around which anthologies can be built. Domestic pets, ships and the sea, the English weather, the pleasures of gardening – the field is limitless. A particularly successful programme of this sort was an anthology of writings about the Devil, broadcast one Hallowe'en.

Full-length novels are regularly abridged into 15-minute instalments for straight reading in such slots as *Woman's Hour* or *A Book at Bedtime*. The writer in this case is faced with carrying out a surgical operation on the original work. First it has to be divided into the number of instalments agreed by the Producer, with each part ending at a suitable point. Then each section msut be pruned to exactly the right length. There may also be a requirement to write short summaries to be read by the announcer at intervals during the transmissions, to bring new listeners up to date in the story. As the original book must not be tampered with but simply shortened there is little creative satisfaction to be gained from this sort of work, and it is not particularly well paid.

Adaptations, however, are a different matter. Some of the best radio drama has come from adaptations of classic novels – Trollope's *Barchester* stories, Galsworthy's *The Forsyte Saga*, Herman Melville's *Moby Dick*, to mention only a few. Here the adapter has to soak himself in the original work and try to enter the mind of its author. The task is to re-create a work written for one medium, be it for the live theatre or the printed page, in terms of another — radio.

Adaptations of stage plays can be fairly straightforward, because the dialogue already exists. Dramatisations of novels, on the other hand, offer more complex problems. Even though the characters may be clearly delineated they have often been given far less actual dialogue than might be expected, and the adapter has to take on the mantle of their original creator in order to make them talk.

Brian Sibley, adapter of J.R. Tolkien's *The Lord of the Rings*, has written eloquently about some of the problems he had to solve:

> Here are just a few facts about the first appearance in the book of some of the major characters (page numbers refer to the one-volume paperback edition): Frodo does not speak until p. 48 ('Has he [Bilbo] gone?'); Sam and Frodo do not appear together until the eavesdropping scene on p. 76; Merry has only two sentences until he meets his companions at the ferry on p. 110; and Gollum does not speak in person until p. 638!
>
> In order to resolve such difficulties — which would clearly be more of a problem for listeners who did not know the book — it seemed necessary to invent some passages of dialogue. A scene was written in which Sam delivers replies to the party invitations to Bilbo and Frodo at Bag End, and another in order to establish Merry before he sets out for Frodo's new home at Crickhollow. And the first episode began with the arrest and interrogation of Gollum by the eerie forces of Mordor (an event which is only reported by Gandalf but which is also referred to in a later Tolkien book, *Unfinished Tales*).
>
> Here, for comparison, is the Merry/Frodo passage from the book, followed by the script:
>
> On September 20th, two covered carts went off laden to Buckland, conveying the furniture and goods that Frodo had not sold. . . . The thought that he [Frodo] would so soon have to part with his young friends weighed on his heart. He wondered how he would break it to them. . . .
>
> The next morning they were busy packing another cart with the remainder of the luggage. Merry took charge of this, and drove off . . . 'Someone must get there and warm the house before you arrive,' said Merry. 'Well, see you later — the day after tomorrow, if you don't go to sleep on the way!'

> **FRODO**: Well, Merry, is everything ready?
> **MERRY**: Yes: two cart-loads yesterday, full to overflowing, and now another one. I'm beginning to wonder if your new home will be big enough!

FRODO: Well, I've sold everything I could bear parting with
to Lobelia, but some things I just had to take to
remind me of Bilbo and Bag End.

MERRY: Well, I'd best be off... If I leave now I can get to
Crickhollow and warm the house before you arrive
— that is, if you're quite sure you want to walk
rather than go by cart...

FRODO: Quite sure.

MERRY: Then I'll see you the day after tomorrow — if you
don't go to sleep on the way!

FRODO: (LAUGHING) I'll try not to!
CART STARTS OFF, THEN STOPS

MERRY: (CALLING BACK) I'll tell you one thing, Frodo, you
had better settle when you get to Buckland, because
I for one am not helping you to move back again!

FRODO: What on earth makes you think Lobelia would ever
sell Bag End back to me?
CART STARTS OFF ONCE MORE

MERRY: She might — at a profit! Farewell, Frodo — and good
walking!
CART DRIVES OFF

FRODO: (TO HIMSELF) Poor Merry, what will you say
when you learn the truth of all this?
FADE

Without offering any serious defence of additions of mock-Tolkien such
as this, the astute reader will observe that, as well as helping establish
Merry's light-hearted personality (he does not appear again until two
episodes later), a variety of information is conveyed, ranging from
details of where they are going and to whom Bag End has been sold, to
a gentle reminder of the existence of Bilbo who left at the end of the
previous episode.

Similar problems occur throughout the book. There are often a large
number of characters present in a scene who do not make any
contribution to the conversations taking place. When reading the book
it matters very little if, for some pages, Gimli or Legolas don't speak,
but on radio a silent character is a non-existent character. These
difficulties come thickest at the end of the book: the struggle at the
Crack of Doom between Frodo and Gollum is, Tolkien tells us, enacted
in silence (except for the odd hiss or two) which is hardly helpful to the
would-be dramatist, and the final partings of the many characters are
woefully short of dialogue. Consider, for example, Frodo's farewell to
Sam: 'Then Frodo kissed Merry and Pippin, and last of all Sam, and went
aboard . . .' Something more was needed for the final parting of the two
heroes whose adventures we have followed for twenty-six weeks.
Simple lines were given to Bilbo, Merry and Pippin, and for Sam and
Frodo some dialogue was transferred from a page before:

FRODO:	Sam ...
SAM:	Oh, Mr Frodo, I thought you were going to enjoy the Shire for years and years, after all you have done.
FRODO:	So I thought too, once. But I have been too deeply hurt, Sam. I tried to save the Shire, and it has been saved, but not for me. It must often be so, Sam, when things are in danger: someone has to give them up, lose them, so that others may keep them. But you are my heir: all that I had and might have had I leave to you, Sam. You will be the most famous gardener in history, and you will read things out of the Red Book, and keep alive the memory of the age that is gone, so that people will remember the Great Danger and so love their beloved land all the more. And that will keep you as busy and as happy as anyone can be, as long as your part of the story goes on ...
SAM:	Oh, Mr Frodo, my dear ... my dear ... THEY KISS
GANDALF:	Now ... Go in peace! I will not say: do not weep; for not all tears are an evil!

(Reprinted from an article in *Mallorn* 17, October 1981)

Although Brian Sibley claims that a silent character is a non-existent character, it is worth recalling a play called *Congress* by Malcolm Bradbury, produced for Afternoon Theatre in November 1981. This centred on the experiences of a Dr Vestey as a delegate to a European Congress to discuss cultural and economic inter-penetration in the 'eighties. Throughout the play Dr Vestey himself never spoke. It was something of a *tour de force* for both writer and producer, but not to my mind entirely successful.

Copyright

Before embarking on making a radio adaptation of an existing work it is as well to check on two important points. Firstly, is the writer of the book, play or story still alive? If so, will he be happy for you to adapt his work? He may well wish to do so himself. If he has died within the past fifty years, copyright clearance will have to be negotiated with the heirs of his estate. If you belong to the Society of Authors they will be able to establish the copyright situation for you. It is unlikely that you, as the writer, will have to foot the bill for copyright payments; this will be the responsibility of the broadcasting company. It is wise, however, for you to be fully informed as to whether copyright negotiations will be necessary before you put up your script proposal.

Secondly, check with the broadcasting company to whom you hope to sell your adaptation that they haven't already produced a version of the same work before, or that they haven't just commissioned someone else to make one. Quite often the same notion can strike several writers and producers at the same time.

Failure to make these essential checks can result in artistic frustration and a lot of wasted work.

7
Comedy and
Light Entertainment

In the days before radio and television music-halls flourished up and down the country. Comedy acts were toured from one place to another round the various circuits. At each town the performers could expect a different audience, who would respond with spontaneous glee to material which, although already well-polished by use elsewhere, was entirely new to them. Those days are long over. A broadcast comedy show is heard by millions – the equivalent of more than a year's tour from town to town – at one performance. The material is then old. No wonder the demand for good comedy writers is so voracious! The ability to see what will make people laugh, and then to set it down on paper, is a precious gift.

The old music-hall formula of a series of miscellaneous acts introduced by a wise-cracking compere has survived in television. Radio, however, has given birth to its own formats which, in the BBC, are the province of the Department of Light Entertainment. This department supplies a whole range of programmes to all four of the national radio networks. Most panel games, quizzes, sketch shows, revue and variety shows, and half-hour comedy series come from Light Entertainment. More surprisingly, most of Radio 2's movie programmes, occasional documentaries with entertainment-based subjects, such as *The Palladium Story*, some light drama series such as *Detective*, *Space Force*, *So Much Blood*, and the Lord Peter Wimsey serials also come from this department.

The key thing to remember is that Light Entertainment Department thinks in terms of series. Any idea that may be submitted to them is assessed on whether or not it might make a series, and if possible a second and third series.

Nearly all series are of half-hour duration. This means in practice 28 minutes, from which 45 seconds are deducted by the requirements of network presentation. Opening and closing announcements, including cast list and writer's credits have to be included within the remaining 27′15″, so that leaves about 26 minutes for the script proper. It's a mistake to send in anything that lasts too long. Read your script aloud at a realistic speed, and cut it ruthlessly to the required length. If you can't, then perhaps you should send it to Drama Department instead.

30-minute comedy drama

Half-hour comedy drama programmes, often loosely called 'sit-coms' (situation comedies), call for a group of characters, more or less believable, to be placed in a situation more or less fantastical. The comedy arises from the interaction between the characters, and the situations in which they find themselves. Sit-com is an aspect of drama, with laughs instead of tension. Each week the same characters recur, but the situation changes. In a play the protagonists develop and change as a result of the experiences they undergo; in sit-com they emerge just the same. The audience tunes in each week to hear them be themselves all over again.

One of the earliest sit-coms was *Bandwagon*, in which Arthur Askey and Richard Murdoch purported to live in a flat on top of Broadcasting House with an assortment of characters including Nausea the goat. Then there was Tommy Handley with *ITMA*, and Jimmy Edwards in *Take it from Here*, with the continuing saga of the Glum family. Tony Hancock reached heights of genius in *Hancock's Half Hour*. More recently, we have had *King Street Junior*, set in a Primary school; *Yes, Minister*, satirising the corridors of power and the machinery of government; and *The Wordsmiths of Gorsemere*, a sophisticated parody on the family life of the poet Wordsworth and his contemporaries. Another series enjoying popular success is *Radio Active*, which travesties the output of a local radio station.

Depending on the nature of the scripts, they may or may not be produced before a live audience. The sort of comedy that produces hearty laughter usually needs the warmth of a human response when it is recorded. The warm-up man does his best to put the audience into a receptive frame of mind before recording starts, and to encourage its members to see themselves as actively contributing to the success of the show, as indeed they do. The mirth you hear punctuating broadcasts of BBC comedy shows is spontaneous and not canned. Shows which rely on a more intellectual approach, tending to evoke quiet chuckles rather than guffaws, are better off without an audience. *The Wordsmiths* is an example.

The elements of comedy

Structure is even more important in a series comedy than in a play. Every episode, and every scene within an episode, must build cumulatively for laughs, starting with a chuckle and ending with a belly laugh that will carry the audience over into the next scene. Successful comedy is created either by performers who are naturally funny, or by straight actors with a good sense of comic timing. Both groups need scripts in order to be able to work their magic. The trick is either to put a funny man in an ordinary situation, or to put an ordinary man in an extraordinary situation. In each case the incongruity between character and situation leads to anarchy, and all good comedy partakes to some extent of anarchy.

Perhaps the supreme example of comic anarchy can be found in the *Goon Show*, originally broadcast between 1951 and 1960, but still brought out of honourable retirement from time to time for nostalgic repeat airings, and still capable of reducing its audience to helplessness. The *Goon Show* team had the advantage of naturally funny men, all capable of playing a number of different parts with highly characteristic voices, plus brilliant scripts written by themselves.

A number of the *Goon Show* scripts have been published in book form, and the writer can learn much from their short lines, economy of language, consistent and clear-cut presentation of the various characters, exploitation of catch-phrases, surrealistic use of effects, and the zany logic which somehow succeeds in creating the radio equivalent of a drawing by Escher. The Goons achieved a level of sublime lunacy which has rarely been equalled.

Panel games and quizzes

Quizzes and panel games are another important element of the Light Entertainment output. These fall into two main categories:

1) Straightforward quizzes in which opposing teams, often drawn from members of the public, compete with each other to answer general knowledge questions. This type of programme relies for its interest on the competitive excitement of whether or not the teams can answer the questions accurately within the time allowed.
Examples: *Brain of Britain, Top of the Form*.

2) Entertainment quizzes and games, which rely on show-business personalities to divert the audience with amusing anecdotes and chat while answering the questions, which are only incidental to the main business of the programme.
Examples: *The News Quiz, My Music, Just a Minute, Wit's End*.

Devising a successful quiz-game format can be a paying proposition, and good ideas for new programmes will be welcomed. *Twenty Questions*, a radio version of an old-time parlour game, was so successful that it ran for years and years, making the reputations of several broadcasting personalities, and a lot of money for its creator. Before you submit a new inspiration however, check on the following points:

a) Is it really original?

b) Does it contain more than a proposal for one round within a programme?

c) Does it ask too much of the contributors? The tasks you want the panellists to undertake should be interesting and entertaining in themselves, and not rely too much on the sparkling chat of the participants – who may, even the best of them, have an off day.

These are among the main reasons for the rejection of suggestions in this field of programming.

Sketches and 'quickies'

If you want to write sketches and 'quickies', study the current output and decide which programmes attract you. By the time a programme is broadcast the whole run will probably have already been recorded, so the likelihood of your being able to contribute to the current series is remote. Your best course is to approach the producer, whose name will be in *Radio Times*, and find out if another series is planned, and if so whether there is scope for outside contributions. For very topical shows such as *Week Ending* and *The News Huddlines*, which use a lot of material from freelance writers, it is more or less essential to live close to the production centre, so that you can attend script meetings and send in specially tailored material at the last minute.

Another approach is to study the work of any comic you particularly admire, put together a batch of short items, and send them to him, with a covering letter saying you would like to write material for him. If he comes to perform in your neighbourhood go to his show, and call on him in his dressing room afterwards. He cannot but be pleased at your interest. Personal contact is worth a lot in show business; enthusiasm and perseverance even more.

Find a partner

Writing comedy is hard work, and lonelier than most forms of writing. As you polish and re-work the lines it is easy to become discouraged and cease to believe that anyone could ever find them funny. A fellow-writer with a similar sense of humour could provide the necessary antidote — someone to laugh at your jokes, to spark you off, to come up with another idea when your mind is a blank. Many superb comedy scripts have been written by partnerships. Muir and Norden, Galton and Simpson, Perry and Crofts, Brady and Bingham are names to conjure with in the business. Perhaps a like-minded colleague might be the answer for you. How do you find one? Join the nearest Writers' Circle.

8
News and Current Affairs

From the earliest days of broadcasting the presentation of up-to-date news has been a major element of radio programming. The capacity to be truly topical gives radio a marked advantage over all other media. Newspapers have to be typeset, printed and distributed. Even television, with its more cumbersome equipment, can only match the flexibility of radio by luck or careful pre-planning. The radio reporter needs no more than a telephone line to feed his story directly into the middle of a news bulletin. Eye and voice are the tools of his trade, closely supported by his trusty tape-recorder.

The best way in to the profession of radio journalism is through a sound education coupled with practical experience gained by contributing to local newspapers and radio stations. There are career openings in this field for both staff and freelance work.

Balance and impartiality

Who decides what is news, and how it should be presented? In Britain the law relating to broadcasting requires that news shall be presented with impartiality and objectivity. Clause 13/7 of the BBC's current licence includes the words:

> The Corporation shall at all times refrain from sending any
> broadcast matter expressing the opinion of the Corporation
> on current affairs or on matters of public policy ...

So, unlike newspapers, broadcasting companies are not permitted to take an editorial line. At one time an attempt was made to balance opposing points of view on controversial topics within individual programmes. This was found to be virtually impossible, and now opposing points of view are presented in different programmes balanced over the output as a whole. Politicians often claim, especially at election times, that the BBC or IBA News is biased against them, but so long as all parties feel equally strongly that they have been the victims the broadcasters believe they have steered a reasonably fair course.

Writing the news

Who actually writes the news? The task is shared between reporters at the coal-face, as it were, and newsroom staff who edit and may re-write a story to fit constraints of time or policy. Many radio journalists start as 'stringers' — local correspondents who telephone the newsroom with a report of an event in their area. Their material may be written up for the news-reader to deliver and their voices never heard on the air. On the other hand, they may find themselves at the heart of a major news story, called on for eyewitness accounts for a whole range of different bulletins, each of which will need a different length and a different style. Compare *News at One* on Radio 4 with *Newsbeat* on Radio 1, or the news as presented on your Local Radio Station, BBC or Independent.

An internal News Guide produced by the BBC for its own staff points out that 'It is a waste of time to broadcast news unless it is listened to and understood. ... Our aim is intelligibility, and what is more, immediate intelligibility.' It goes on to recommend 'a style that is crisp, economical, direct and colloquial, but not slangy or slap-dash, relaxed yet precise. We prefer the short word to the long one, the simple sentence to the complex, the concrete to the abstract, the direct statement to the inverted sentence. We do not write for pedants. But we shun journalese.'

Two books which may be especially helpful in connection with news and current affairs writing are R.W. Burchfield's *The Spoken Word, A BBC Guide* and *The Complete Plain Words* by Sir Ernest Gowers, revised by Sidney Greenbaum and Janet Whitcut.

News versus comment

Ideally, a distinction should be made between news — what actually happened — and comment, which is a response to or interpretation of what happened. In practice it is extremely difficult to draw a line between the two. The very selection of items for inclusion in a bulletin and the order in which they are placed constitutes comment of a sort. It behoves the radio journalist to be scrupulously careful in his choice of vocabulary not to imply any sort of judgement where none is intended. A word such as 'freedom fighter' carries an overtone of approval, while 'terrorist' suggests the opposite. 'Gunman' might serve for either. To say 'Troops were forced to open fire' is to imply a subjective opinion that there was no alternative. 'Troops opened fire' is a neutral statement.

Meticulous accuracy is essential in all reporting, and this extends to sources and attributions. 'The Labour/Conservative group on the

Council have succeeded in convincing their opponents of the necessity
...' might more accurately be reported as 'The Labour/Conservative
group on the Council *say* they have succeeded in convincing ...'. If
'say' were replaced by 'maintain', or 'assert', or 'claim', any of these
alternative words would carry its own connotation of credibility – or
the reverse.

Interviews

Interviews form an important element in news reports. The reporter
has to use his own skill with words to set a scene and bring it to life for
the listener, and then efface himself by eliciting as much of the story as
possible from the key people involved.

Interviewing is both a skill and an art. The interviewer must have a
clear idea of the purpose of his recording and the length of time it will
eventually be allowed to run. Interviews in news bulletins usually have
to be short and to the point. The reporter must evoke factual responses
and avoid leading questions which allow simple 'yes' or 'no' replies.
Thus, not:

> Q. Mr Jones, I believe you were standing in the doorway
>   when the thunderbolt fell?
> A. Yes.

but:

> Q. Mr Jones, where were you when the thunderbolt fell?
> A. Standing in the doorway. . . .

In slotting a recording into the rest of the programme the interviewer's
first question is often cut. The extract above might be introduced as
follows:

> Newsreader: A thunderbolt struck a shop in Little
>   Mudhampton this morning. Our reporter asked
>   Fred Jones the shopkeeper where he was when
>   it fell.
> Tape insert: 'Standing in the doorway . . .'

Some interviewees are fluent talkers. One question unleashes a graphic
description of their experiences. Others have to be prompted. The
interviewer should never, ever comment. He should avoid remarks
such as 'How interesting', 'Did it really?', or 'No!' A radio interview is
not a social conversation. Instead of reacting as if it were, the
interviewer should simply go on to the next question.

The interviewee should not be interrupted as this will make for
difficult editing. The interviewer may want to eliminate his own voice

from the final version and present the answers to a series of questions as continuous statement. If both speak at once this will be impossible.

The purpose of the interview may not be a topical report for a news bulletin. Perhaps it is a profile of someone in the public eye, and time has been allocated for an extended 'personality' piece. Now, although the foregoing remarks still apply, you can afford to be more leisurely in your approach. Research your subject thoroughly beforehand. Plan an over-all structure, with a good opening and close. Prepare a list of questions. If possible, get to know your interviewee beforehand and gain his confidence. Agree the areas to be covered in your discussion, but never under any circumstances rehearse. If you do, you may find your interviewee trying to remember what he said last time, or using expressions such as 'Well, as I said before . . .'. You may want to make a short trial recording to check microphone balance, but ask a totally unconnected question such as 'What did you have for breakfast this morning?'.

There are several ways of encouraging people to go on talking into a tape recorder, but they have to be non-verbal. You must not say 'Yes?', 'Mmm?', or 'Go on'. Your best tool is eye-contact. Rivet your victim with your fascinated gaze and convince him that you are deeply interested in what he is saying. As long as you nod enthusiastically at intervals he will go on elaborating his story. When he comes to a halt, just remain silently expectant. People find it very difficult not to fill a silence, and probably something more will be forthcoming. If your tape has pauses in it you can easily edit them out afterwards.

On the whole it is wiser not to play recordings back to people after they have been interviewed. Often time does not allow for this, but even if it does people are sometimes dissatisfied with recordings and you may find yourself pressed to re-do the whole thing, or cut various passages – perhaps the very ones which you feel to be most effective. This is not to say that answers to some questions should not be re-recorded at the request of either interviewer or interviewee. When you come to edit the recording, integrity requires that you present what your interviewee said in the light that he intended, using your professional skill and judgement to compile the most effective end product.

Commentating

Radio's capacity to bring the listener reports of events while they are actually happening has led to the rise of the professional commentator. Ball-by-ball accounts of cricket matches and the thrills of Wimbledon tennis are regularly relayed in word pictures to the listening millions.

Associated noises – the thwack of ball on bat or racket, the roar of the crowd – add to the impression of actuality, but the main burden falls on the speaker's voice. This is even more true of ceremonial public occasions such as the opening of Parliament, Trooping the Colour, or a Royal Wedding. The commentator has to keep talking, come what may.

Successful commentaries require immense and detailed preparation. All those long moments when nothing is happening – the batsman is walking out to the wicket, the start of the race is delayed, the Royal carriage has not yet appeared – must be filled with colourful and appropriate talk. The commentator must make himself familiar with every relevant fact, so that he can drop it in at some empty and unforgiving minute. When the action resumes he must transform himself into a sort of tap from which an account of the passing scene pours like water, bringing the listener vivid vicarious experience. He must share in and communicate the excitement of the occasion, but remain sufficiently in command of himself to be articulate and lucid.

Over the years commentators have come to use a technique called the Pyramid Method – clearly expounded in Brian Johnson's book *My Friends the Commentators*. The Commentator starts his broadcast at the tip of the pyramid by giving immediately the main essentials of the situation. Then, gradually as the broadcast continues, he can broaden outwards by adding less important but still relevant information. In quiet pauses in the flow of events the commentator can draw on what is called 'associative' material – the history of the occasion, the significance of the uniforms, or perhaps a personal anecdote. He should, nevertheless, remember to weave in a description of the scene again from time to time, and repeat essential information, such as the current score in a cricket or football match, for the benefit of new listeners who may have just tuned in.

Two important 'don'ts' for commentators – never admit you can't see even if it's true, and don't take sides. Your listeners will include people of all sympathies and nationalities.

Brian Johnson tells the story of the ace Canadian commentator Stewart MacPherson, preparing for a broadcast on a firework display by filling a blank sheet of paper with every adjective he thought he might want to use – brilliant, fantastic, magnificent, sparkling, and so-on. As the display went on he struck each adjective out as he used it, and so cut down on the inevitable repetitions.

If you dream of becoming a sports commentator you could start by writing up reports of matches for a school magazine or local newspaper. You could practice by watching a match on television with the sound turned down, and recording your own commentary. Play the tape back later, and see how much of a sound picture you gave of what actually happened. Then tackle the sports editor at your local radio station to see if he will give you a trial.

The best commentators sometimes get carried away in the stress of the moment, and the satirical magazine *Private Eye* has immortalised one of them by producing anthologies of some of their wilder malapropisms under the title *Colemanballs*. One of my favourites — not, as it happens, by David Coleman — is reproduced below.

And a sedentary seagull flies by . . .

BRIAN JOHNSTON

Colemanballs II (Private Eye/André Deutsch)

9
Educational and Information Programmes

The potential of radio as a medium of education was recognised early. By 1926 nearly 2000 schools in Britain were listening to radio programmes. School broadcasting was not, however, greeted with unmixed enthusiasm. There were a number of worries, including the fear that radio might supplant the classroom teacher and lead to loss of jobs in the profession. This was ironic, because it quickly became apparent that school broadcasts depended closely on co-operation at the receiving end for their success. Listening to the radio was not an easy option for the teacher.

The BBC was anxious for advice from the educational world on how to proceed, and in 1927 the Carnegie Trustees financed a major enquiry in collaboration with the Kent Advisory Committee of Teachers and the Kent Education Committee. The famous 'Kent Experiment' resulted in a report called *Educational Broadcasting* which has had an enduring influence on policy.

Essential partnership

The most important point to emerge was the necessity of establishing a close partnership between broadcasters and educationists. This led to the setting up of the School Broadcasting Council which, through a network of sub-committees, was to 'commission' the BBC to provide broadcasts designed to fulfil clearly defined purposes for different target audiences. In other words, the BBC would plan its educational output in response to direct requests from representative advisory bodies. This principle still holds good, and leads to the corollary that — certainly in network radio — educational material is almost invariably commissioned.

A second key recommendation was that broadcasting should concentrate on offering the audience material and experiences which could not be provided by the teacher in the classroom. Although the press might refer to 'lessons on the air' the BBC School Broadcasting Department leaned over backwards to dispel notions that it was providing any such thing. The radio was seen as providing an extra resource for the teacher, a stimulus to the imagination, which could be drawn on to enrich the normal curriculum. The teacher's role in the classroom was paramount, and nothing would be done to usurp it.

Today the BBC is regarded as a major provider of educational material for all ages – infants, primary and secondary school-children, students at universities and Polytechnics, and adults who want to go on learning. The greatly extended School Broadcasting Council has been joined by an Advisory Council for Continuing Education. The School Broadcasting Departments, both Radio and Television, still work to commissions handed down by the SBC, but the emphasis on avoiding infringement on the teacher's role has been greatly modified.

Tape recording for self access

Some 92% of all primary schools listen to school radio programmes, most of them at the time they are transmitted. The development of tape recording, however, has made it possible to use broadcasts in new ways. Many programmes intended for secondary audiences are now broadcast after midnight, so that schools can set time switches and record them *en bloc* for subsequent listening at convenient opportunities. Some series are even designed specifically for students to use by themselves, listening on their own cassette recorders, without the teacher's presence (e.g. *Help Yourself*). This means that the former pattern of a weekly series of 20-minute self-contained programmes topped and tailed with announcements has given way to a more flexible, magazine-type approach, providing resource material which can be drawn on at will. This calls for writers who also have skills as interviewers and presenters.

One lesson which has been learned by the broadcasters is that radio on its own is a bird with a broken wing. It needs support, perhaps from printed publications, or from computer software, or ideally from a real live teacher who can help and stimulate. The techniques of distance-learning are highly effective over limited periods of time, but the spirit takes fire with human contact and encouragement.

Qualifications for educational broadcasters

It is not essential to be a teacher in order to write for educational radio. It is important, however, to know and understand the audience for whom you are writing, and to be familiar with current educational thinking and practice in the appropriate subject area. In presenting new information and ideas you must know what your audience has already learned, and put over your material in terms that they will understand.

If you find yourself wanting to use an expression that will be unfamiliar to them, various alternatives present themselves. First, ask yourself what the main objective is of this particular broadcast, and whether it is essential for this expression to be used at this point in the course. If not, find a way of re-phrasing your script so as to avoid it, otherwise you run the risk of blocking understanding of the rest of what you are saying. If your listeners do need to learn it, you can either explain it there and then, or make sure, through supporting printed notes, that an explanation has been given to them before the broadcast.

The schools audience is particularly rewarding for two reasons. Firstly, you will be given a clear brief to work to, so you will know exactly what the broadcast is intended to achieve. Secondly, there will be positive feed-back afterwards from the listening end. This is somewhat different from the general output, where – unless you have a sensational hit or a scandal on your hands – you may wonder who, if anyone at all, listened to your broadcast.

The annual programme

The school broadcasting output receives only limited coverage in *Radio Times*. The documents with all the information are the Annual Programmes, separate for primary and secondary, which are sent out to schools and colleges in July of each year. From these you will gain an insight into the many carefully devised series which are planned, commissioned, produced and broadcast by the School Radio and Television Departments.

The Annual Programme distributed in July covers the projected output for the whole of the next academic year. These plans were approved by the School Broadcasting Council in June of the previous year, so the schedule works on a rolling two-year cycle. In June 1987 the SBC approved plans for programmes in the year September 1988/June 1989; in June 1988, programmes will be approved for the year September 1989/June 1990; and so on. This extended time-scale is necessary so that broadcasts can be prepared in step with related publications – notes for teachers, pamphlets for pupils and the rest – and so that schools can be provided with full information in time to draw up their own timetables and order the appropriate support materials before the start of each academic year.

Openings for freelances

It will be seen, therefore, that any school broadcast is the fruit of a long period of gestation. It is largely a waste of time to send in unsolicited scripts designed as part of the current output. Decisions may have been taken to scrap or modify an established series, or to introduce something new and different. What you are listening to now was almost certainly commissioned some time ago. Nevertheless, not everything is sewn up tight. There are openings for freelance contributions, and producers are glad to hear from people interested in writing for the school audience. Fewer plays are commissioned nowadays, but particularly in programmes for infants and juniors, there is a market for stories and poetry. New approaches in drama and music also offer scope for writers. *Music Workshop*, aimed at children of 8 and over, presents musical plays suitable for school performance, and skill in lyric-writing could be welcomed here. If you want to contribute to school radio, write either to the producer of a series which interests you, or to the Executive Producer of School Broadcasting, Radio, stating your interest and experience with the audience and enclosing a sample of your work. This need not be anything written for radio, so long as it gives an impression of the quality of your writing.

Adult education

The BBC Open University Production Centre at Milton Keynes was set up to produce the radio and television components of all the Open University courses. In addition it has now gained a considerable reputation as a national resource for the origination of audio-visual training materials, and is rapidly developing special expertise in the field of inter-active video disc production. Medical Schools in particular have taken advantage of this special area of excellence.

BBC educational programmes for adults come under the department of Continuing Education (Radio). Here there has been a trend away from groups of programmes intended to be received by a class, towards 'educative' programmes designed to be listened to by individuals at home. The output of this department is not so closely tied to commissions from its advisory council, and the time-scale of its operations is consequently not quite so extended. It is responsible for *Options* on Radio 4, broadcast on Saturday and Sunday afternoons, and for the various language teaching courses. It also puts out series of programmes designed to improve understanding of the wider world, for example Gerald Butt on *The Arab World*, and Hugh O'Shaughnessy's *Mexican Journey*. Other areas in which the Continuing Education Department has been active have included industrial relations, the environment, and a national food and health campaign. BBC External Services have achieved world-wide renown in the language-teaching field with *English by Radio*.

Educational radio in the wider world

The BBC's knowledge and expertise in the field of educational broadcasting is in demand throughout the world, and many foreign institutions send students to this country for BBC training courses. This country is fortunate in being well provided with good schools and trained teachers. It can afford to regard the broadcasting media almost as a luxury, to be used or not as educationists may choose. In third world countries, however, where schools are scattered and ill-equipped and perhaps even the teachers have only had a limited education, radio is a vital resource. Broadcasting can spread understanding of new farming techniques, health education, and many more topics of vital interest in helping developing communities to achieve fuller and happier lives.

In developed countries with western traditions, such as Australia and New Zealand, radio is also a life-line over long distances. Educational programmes, both for school children and adults, are an important part of broadcasting output. In Australia *Schools of the Air* are run by each state for children in isolated communities. Teachers at central studios teach their far-flung classes by two-way conversation, using the technology of interactive radio.

Religious broadcasting

Radio is a powerful selling medium, and its capacity to put over a message has been exploited for good and ill. It has been used to sell soap-powder and Fascism, to convey information and to preach religious creeds. The development of radio has coincided with great changes in education and society. When the BBC started broadcasting in the 1920s, religion to most of its listeners meant Christianity. The daily service and *Thought for the Day* remain as reminders of that state of affairs. Religious broadcasting in today's multi-cultural society has a much wider connotation. The religious affairs producer may commission plays, features, or talks and discussions of all sorts, reflecting all the principal faiths now being practised in this country and around the world. Ideas from thoughtful writers will find a warm response in this field. Local radio plays a particularly important part in religious broadcasting, and the speakers are not only vicars and priests. Many distinguished speakers and producers have graduated to national networks from the proving ground of low-budget local radio programmes. Limitations often provide the best stimulus for truly creative and imaginative work, and this is certainly true in the field of religious affairs.

10
Audio-Visual Scripts

An interesting spin-off from educational radio has been dubbed 'radiovision'. The technique was first developed during the early 'sixties, but still forms part of the school broadcasting armoury. Radiovision scripts are commissioned as part of a school broadcasting series in the same way as other scripts. A radiovision programme is a sound-track designed to be complemented by a set of slides or a filmstrip. Schools play the tape and project the accompanying pictures simultaneously, in their own time. This is not the same thing as the simultaneous broadcasting of a television programme on sound radio, which has also been called radio-vision.

The hybrid tape-slide medium has valuable advantages over both radio and television for certain applications. Projected slides can provide bigger, better pictures for a class than the television screen. Both television and film abhor a still picture, whereas a slide can be held on the screen for as long as may be desirable. Visual material in a programme can be updated cheaply and easily by substituting fresh slides. In programmes dealing with historical subjects slides can often show actual contemporary pictures, whereas television or film producers may be driven to resort to reconstructions or library footage which may not be authentic.

One of the most notable examples of this was a radiovision programme first broadcast twenty or more years ago called *In the Trenches*. The script, by John Chilton, told the story of the First World War through quotations from letters, poems, memoirs, and above all the popular songs sung by the soldiers themselves. The filmstrip showed posters, newspaper reports, and actual contemporary photographs of daily life in the trenches. The interplay between the black humour of the soldiers' ballads with their relentlessly cheerful tunes and the grim images of the muddy carnage in Flanders resulted in an experience of overwhelming irony and pathos. Truly the whole was far greater than the sum of its parts. This school history programme, still repeated from time to time, achieved immortality in fresh incarnations on stage and screen as *Oh What a Lovely War!*.

In the Trenches was a simple programme in which a single projector was used and the film-strip frames changed by hand. If extra projectors are brought in and a computer employed to synchronise them with the sound-track a sophisticated result can be achieved which is very close to moving-picture film. Slides can be mixed, dissolved, superimposed and split-screened with dazzling virtuosity. The advertising world has taken this technique to its heart, and elaborate 'audio-visuals' to extol the virtues of new products and services are now a recognised element of glossy PR presentations. If you are interested in writing for this market try approaching an advertising agency or one of the independent audio-visual production companies.

Video-tape and interactive video-disc are increasingly coming into use for training applications, but not only are they expensive to produce, they require a reliable source of electric power. The simple tape-slide programme is still a highly efficient and economical medium of instruction and information, much used in the tourist industry and in medical and health education. An organisation called TALC (Teaching Aids at Low Cost) specialises in originating tape-slide programmes for the third world. The BMA's Audio Visual Communications Department at Blatt House in London acts as a show-case for their wares, and also for those produced by the Graves Medical Audio Visual Library at Chelmsford, and by universities and medical schools all over the country.

Script-writing methods

In writing a script for this sort of presentation it is important to achieve a balance between pictures and talk. Which should come first, the slides or the commentary? This question is often asked, and the answer is that they have to come together. Start with a blank A4 page, divided vertically in two. Down the left-hand side list the pictures you have, or hope to obtain. In the right-hand half, set down the proposed commentary. If you find yourself with a full page of speech and only one picture to go with it there is something wrong with your script. Modify the commentary, add some more pictures, and establish a close interplay between sound and vision.

How to signal the change from one slide to the next can offer problems. A distinctive sound can be used, such as the 'ting' of a bell; or you can write the signal into the script, and get your commentator to say 'Now move on to slide 4', or something similar. On the other hand, if your programme is not openly didactic but designed to convey an aesthetic experience this sort of instruction destroys any atmosphere you may have built up. The alternative is to supply the user with a detailed copy of the script with clear instructions as to the slide changes. Electronic synchronisers are available which will put pulses on the magnetic tape, thus ensuring that the slides are changed automatically at the right points.

Tape-slide programmes are well-suited to self-access use, and many educational libraries have booths where students can work individually with this sort of material. Visualise how your audience will eventually use the script you are working on and, if appropriate, write in instructions such as 'Now switch me off, and work through the next example. Switch on again when you are ready.'

This book does not set out to deal with visual presentation, but one point should be remembered when choosing illustrations for slide-tape programmes: select landscape-shape pictures rather than those of upright format. It's a small point, but one that is often overlooked, and makes a great deal of difference to the finished result.

11
Radio for Children

Between the dark and the daylight,
When the night is beginning to lower,
Comes a pause in the day's occupations
That is known as the children's hour

These lines by Longfellow gave a title to the first radio programmes specially for children, which grew up in parallel with but quite separate from broadcasts for schools. Throughout the golden age of radio the time between 5.0 pm and the six o'clock news was dominated by programmes for younger listeners. *Children's Hour* was a microcosm of BBC output as a whole. Stories, music, quizzes and competitions, plays and features of top quality were produced by organisers in each of the seven main BBC regions.

Children's Hour became a marvellous proving ground for broadcasters of all sorts. Fees were lower than those offered for contributions to the rest of the output, and some of the finest productions were achieved on shoe-string budgets, through real dedication on the part of producers, writers and performers.

The audience was just as dedicated, and included a large number of adult devotees. This is not surprising when one considers what they were offered. Dramatisations of all the classic children's books, including *Wind in the Willows*, *Winnie the Pooh* and *The House at Pooh Corner*; lots of Dickens and Kipling; John Masefield's *Box of Delights* and Frances Hodgson Burnett's *The Secret Garden*; original plays by writers such as Geoffrey Household, Kathleen Fidler and Geoffrey Trease, and immortal creations such as *Toytown* and *Worzel Gummidge*.

But society was changing. Children were staying up later, mothers were going out to work. The days of nannies and nursery tea were long over. Television had arrived, and young listeners were becoming viewers, or choosing their radio fare from the general output. In 1964 the axe fell, and the BBC abolished *Children's Hour*. Some have never forgiven this act of vandalism.

A quarter of a century later there is some sign that an entertainment programme specially for children may be introduced again. There have been experimental runs of a magazine called *Cat's Whiskers* in the mornings during school holidays. Unfortunately, an audience is more easily killed off than re-established. To do this calls for unswerving commitment over a long period of time, and at the moment such commitment seems to be lacking in the BBC network controllers. It does seem ironic that, while both BBC and Independent Television make generous provision for children and most local radio stations take account of the interests of their younger listeners, the BBC national networks, flagship of all that is best in world radio, have been so reluctant to do so.

An early-evening programme that was originally planned for an adult audience but hit the jackpot with older children was *Dick Barton, Special Agent*. Geoffrey Webb and Neil Tuson's book *The Inside Story of Dick Barton* gives some interesting insights into the birth and development of this 15-minute daily adventure serial. When parents and teachers began to realise that schoolchildren were glued to their radio sets at 6.45 pm instead of getting on with their homework all sorts of concerns began to be voiced as to the undesirable influences that Dick Barton might be exerting. It was a straightforward entertainment programme, and therefore not subject to any of the restraints which might have been imposed by a School Broadcasting Council sub-committee. The production team nevertheless found that they had to take careful account of the fact that the broadcasts went straight into the heart of people's homes, where they were lapped up like mother's milk by a young and impressionable audience. A code of conduct was devised to which the writers learned meticulously to adhere. Here are the 'Thirteen commandments':

1. Barton is intelligent as well as hard-hitting.
2. He uses force only when normal peaceful means have failed.
3. Barton never commits an offence under the criminal code, no matter how desirable the end may be to justify the means.
4. In reasonable circumstances Barton may deceive, but he never lies.
5. Barton's violence is restricted to clean socks on the jaw. Refinements of unarmed combat tried by British Commandos cannot be practised by him or his colleagues.
6. His enemies have more latitude in behaviour, but may not inflict any injury or punishment which is basically sadistic.
7. Barton and his colleagues do not wittingly involve members of the public in circumstances which would cause them distress.
8. Barton has given up drink altogether.

9. Sex plays no part in his adventures. He has no flirtations or affairs, and his enemies have no 'molls' or mistresses.
10. Political themes are unpopular as well as being occasionally embarrassing.
11. Horrific effects must be closely watched. Supernatural or pseudo-supernatural sequences involving ghosts, night-prowling gorillas, vampires and so on should be avoided.
12. Swearing may not be used by any character.
13. Neither Barton and his colleagues, nor his opponents may use cut-throat razors, or any other sharp instrument commonly found in private houses for the purpose of causing injury, or for intimidation.

This is probably a fairly sound code for writing material for a school-age audience even in the 1980s, though nowadays one would need, sadly, to add an extra admonition concerning drugs.

Pre-school age children have received a better deal from BBC radio than their older brothers and sisters. *Listen With Mother*, started in 1950, still survives in truncated form as *Listening Corner*, ten minutes in term-time and five minutes in the holidays, Radio 4 VHF/FM, just before two o'clock, Monday to Friday throughout the year. There are openings here for unsolicited scripts, and the standard is high. Jean Sutcliffe, who started *Listen With Mother*, used to speak with scorn of 'baby doggery', and intellectual types who wrote for the rarefied reaches of Radio 3 did not consider contributing to *Listen With Mother* beneath their dignity. A story for this audience needs the elements that make for any successful radio story: a clear narrative, simple, speakable language, a beginning, a middle and an end.

Local radio stations, both BBC and ILR, are interested in attracting young listeners. Devon Air includes a section called *School's Out* in its afternoon magazine every weekday; Ocean Sound at Southampton broadcasts a daily children's story; 2CR at Bournemouth has a regular spot for under-fives in Geoff Allen's *Afternoon Show*; Downtown Radio in Belfast has a two-hour programme on Sunday mornings aimed at five- to fifteen-year olds, and many other local stations run phone-ins, quizzes, competitions and games, with a liberal admixture of pop music, specially designed for the younger members of the audience. Ideas for contributions to these programmes which fit the style of the station will undoubtedly be received with interest.

Participation is a great audience-puller, and children respond quickly to programmes which they recognise as being specially directed to them. They develop a fiercely possessive attitude towards them, and listen with critical appreciation. *Children's Hour* always had a massive postbag, full of all sorts of comments, complaints and requests. To those who are concerned for the quality of radio, a committed audience seems to be the most important factor in assuring a flourishing future. Surely, above all, it is important to nourish and encourage that audience while it is young.

It is interesting to note that the commercial world of audio-publishing has been quick to recognise the demand among children for stories to be read aloud. Every supermarket carries a display of children's audio-cassettes, and aspiring writers of children's stories could do worse than approach some of the production companies involved.

12
Markets, Fees and Copyright

All writers who want to be paid for their work have to learn how to market it, and be prepared to spend time doing so. Marketing means more than just salesmanship. It means identifying a possible purchaser, finding out exactly what that purchaser usually buys, tailoring your product to fit the specification, and presenting it in as attractive and professional a way as possible.

If you want to write for radio there is no substitute for listening to the way successful people have done it. Plays, short stories and comedy programmes are increasingly becoming available on tape, and in some cases the scripts have been published in book form as well. Try listening to a tape and following the written text at the same time. This not only illustrates different writing techniques, it reveals the contribution skilled acting can make in lifting bare words off the page and bringing a situation to life. A list of tapes and published texts will be found at the end of this book.

Looking for possible markets

This book has been written from the standpoint of the United Kingdom, where the BBC dominates the freelance market. There are many other broadcasting stations in the world, however, besides those run by the BBC. Across the Irish Sea in Dublin Radio Telefis Eireann welcomes talks, short stories, features and plays. Guide-lines for radio-writers are available on request. Consider the Commonwealth. In Australia, for instance, there is much more radio at every level than there is in the UK. The Australian Broadcasting Corporation provides television and radio programmes in the national broadcasting service and operates Radio Australia. While ABC radio is interested mainly in contributors with an Australian background, new material of high quality from overseas sources will be considered, submitted either in script or taped form. Radio New Zealand has three public radio networks, of which one is commercial, and a limited shortwave service directed primarily to the Southwest Pacific and Southeastern Australia. New Zealanders are enthusiastic gardeners and deeply interested in anything to do with the countryside. They have been among the most devoted listeners to *The Archers*. Radio plays an important part in the cultural and educational life of India.

Study the list of addresses at the end of this book for other possible markets. Wherever you live in the world you are within reach of radio. Explore the air waves and see how many different stations you can hear. Listen to the sort of material they broadcast, identify a programme you enjoy, and think what sort of a contribution you might make yourself. Follow this up by writing to the station concerned and asking for information about their schedules. They will probably respond with publicity material which will give you some names of producers, executives and presenters. When you have a proposal to put forward you can then address it to someone by name, rather than sending it off into the impersonal blue.

It is essential to study your market, and aim your work carefully at a target slot. The BBC, for example, is a vast organisation and the programme side is divided into many different sections, which may supply material to any or all of its four main networks. It is not enough to address your script BBC, LONDON and hope that they will find the right destination for it. The *Radio Times* will give you names of producers and editors and a clue as to where different programmes were originated. Different BBC Regions tend to develop their own special areas of excellence. BBC Bristol has become renowned in the field of wild life and natural history; BBC Manchester has an outstanding record in bringing forward new playwrights; BBC Birmingham has always had a strong interest in farming.

National and Regional Production Centres, as well as originating their own local material, are often called upon for productions with specialised requirements. For example, a play which needs a Scottish or Welsh cast may be sent to Radio Scotland or Radio Wales for production, even though it was originally submitted to the Drama Script Unit in London. There is thus a two-way traffic between London and the various production centres, and if you live out of London it may be advantageous to send your script to a local producer.

Local Radio stations are a good deal smaller and simpler in their organisation. They usually have key members of staff who take responsibility for broad areas of programme material. There will be a News Editor, a Sports Editor, perhaps an Educational Producer, and so on. They may or may not be people you hear on the air. A telephone call will give you the name of the right person to approach with a script or a programme idea.

The pattern of local radio programming is built on 'sequences', chunks of time in which a presenter sits at the microphone and introduces music, phone-ins, news, interviews and all sorts of miscellaneous items in a continuous 'seamless' flow. Few contributions last longer than three or four minutes. If you can offer interesting material which will fit in with the style of the station they will be delighted to hear from you. There may be little or no payment, but it will give you a chance to build up a track record. Through a programme-sharing scheme selected ILR items are exchanged between stations, and the BBC too has a national showcase for excerpts from their local radio output. This means that your work could reach a wider audience than your immediate area, and come to the notice of other producers. It also means that, when you send a script or an idea to a national network, you can say in your covering letter that you have been working for local radio. This is evidence of serious commitment, and may help to open a door for you. Experience with Hospital Broadcasting, or Talking Newspapers for the Blind can also help to give you valuable experience.

One of the oldest radio stations in Europe is Radio Luxembourg, which has been broadcasting daily programmes in English and the main European languages for more than sixty years. They are open to any suggestions – mainly pop-music oriented – which will fit in with their style of programming and attract an audience. It is worth remembering that many of the best known quiz and game shows now on television started on Radio Luxembourg, as did all the most famous disc jockeys. It regards itself as a station for the young, and is particularly glad to receive ideas from seventeen to eighteen-year-olds, especially if they want to become radio journalists.

'But what if they pinch my idea and use it without telling me?' This frequently-voiced concern takes us into the field of copyright law.

Copyright

There is no copyright in ideas. What is more, there is no copyright in a title, although there are occasions when the use of a title can be restrained. If you discuss your creative thoughts with other people they are perfectly free to make what use they like of them. The moral of this is that you should not talk about your ideas, but write them down. *Once you have given your inspiration written form as a script or a programme format, that expression of your idea is protected by copyright*, and it is illegal to make use of it without your agreement. You do not need to complete any formalities to obtain this protection in the UK, or in any country which is a member of the Berne Copyright Union. Most of the principal countries of the world belong to this Union, with the important exceptions of the USA, the USSR, China, and some of the South American republics. If at the end of your work you add the notice © followed by your name and the year of completion your script will be protected in all the countries which belong to the Universal Copyright Convention, which *does* include the USA and the USSR.

There is a fair amount of evidence for the existence of a climate of ideas, which leads to several people thinking along the same lines simultaneously. It is hard to prove who had an idea first, unless a dated script is there to refer to. In order to prove when you submitted your play/format/sketch, you can if you like place a sealed copy in the care of your bank, and obtain a dated receipt for it, or post a copy to yourself at the same time as you despatch it to the broadcasting company. Plagiarism is difficult to prove, but notable actions at law have been brought and won. If you belong to either the Society of Authors or the Writers Guild they will advise you if you have a case and help you to fight it.

When a company pays for your work it only buys a licence to broadcast it the number of times specified in the contract. The copyright remains your property. Suppose one of your short stories is accepted for the *Morning Story* slot. You are perfectly free to sell the serial rights to a magazine, to adapt it as a play for radio, television or the theatre, or to make whatever further use you choose of your own copyright material. Re-cycling of previously written material can be profitable, and for this reason writers should never throw anything away. An idea may fail at first because the moment is not right for it. Two or three years later the situation may be different. Producers and editors change, and so does the climate of ideas. A word of warning, though: the BBC keeps a comprehensive record of all playscripts ever submitted, with comments. So if you want to have another go with one that has been rejected, re-work it thoroughly and give it a fresh title before you send it in again.

Fees

What can you expect to earn? That depends who you are selling to. In Britain the main purchaser of freelance scripted material is the BBC. BBC producers do not talk money. That task is delegated to administrative departments which deal with contracts and copyright. The producer will send a requisition to the appropriate department saying that he wants to commission you, say, to write and deliver a 5-minute talk on brass monkeys for *Woman's Hour*. The talks bookings department will then offer you a contract based on a scale of fees agreed with the Writers Guild and the Society of Authors. You can either accept this, or if you are dissatisfied argue for more money, without sullying relations with your producer. Ideally, contracts should be received before the work is done, and certainly before the broadcast takes place, but in the case of topical material this often doesn't happen. *Be wary of something called an ARR contract.* This stands for All Radio Rights, and means just that. If you sign it you will not be entitled to any repeat fees however many times the material is used on however many of the BBC's services. It is a form of contract intended for short contributions likely to be of ephemeral interest, and not exceeding an air time of 5 minutes, for which you will not be expected to have undertaken any research.

Scales of fees are revised from time to time, so the following list can be regarded only as an indication. It is drawn from the October 1987 edition of the Society of Authors Broadcasting Bulletin.

BBC minimum rates 1987

Radio Drama
Established writers: £23.10 per minute
Beginners: £15.25 per minute

Attendance payment
There is a single payment of £23.10 per production to cover all attendances which a writer may make at rehearsals or recordings. Only established writers are eligible for this.

Pension Contributions
Writers who are members of the Society of Authors or the Writers Guild are entitled to receive an additional sum equivalent to 5% of their initial fee. The sum, together with a further sum equivalent to 3% of the initial fee, which shall be set aside as the writer's contribution from the initial fee, will be paid by the BBC to the Guild/Society pension fund for the credit of the writer.

Dramatisations
In offering fees for dramatisations the BBC uses the following guidelines:

a) For dramatisations which draw on the original not only for the basic construction but also for most of the dialogue, 60% of the full drama rate would be appropriate.

b) For dramatisations which draw on the original for the basic construction but where more than half the dialogue has to be invented by the dramatiser, 75% of the full drama rate would be appropriate.

c) For dramatisations which require the dramatiser to

undertake major structural changes and to invent more than half the dialogue, 85% of the full rate would be appropriate.

Abridgements

The rates paid for abridgements are now equivalent to 20% of the drama rate. The established writer's going rate for abridgements is £4.62 per minute, and beginners are paid a minimum rate of £3.05 per minute.

School Cassette Service

The BBC will pay 10% of the initial fee (or the current fee if the rights are taken up after the school year in which the work is first transmitted) as an advance against a royalty of 4% of the published retail price (exclusive of VAT) of each cassette sold.

Talks and Features

The following minimum rates apply to the domestic and external services:

Interviewers (ARR contracts)	£34.90
Interviewers (Talks Requisition Contract)	
Up to 5 minutes	£30.40
5–8 minutes	£35.35
8–12 minutes	£42.65
12 minutes and over	negotiable
Script and read	£12.45 per minute
Script only	£9.15 per minute
Illustrated talks	£10.20 per minute
Linked interviews	
1 interview	£54.90
2 interviews	£71.15

NB The minimum fee for script and reading and script only contributions is two minutes. For illustrated talks the minimum is three minutes.

Features and Documentaries

The normal rate is £109.90 for up to 7 minutes, and then £16.50 per minute. More may be paid to very experienced contributors. Special high fees will be offered when justified by the particular circumstances of the engagement.

Interviewees

The fees paid to interviewees are not negotiated with the unions. Interviewees on ARR (All Radio Rights) contracts are paid £23.00. The contracts are used for short contributions likely to be of ephemeral interest, and not exceeding an air time of five minutes. The contributor will not be expected to have engaged in research for the contribution.

Repeats

Repeats of contributions covered by the Talks Requisition Contract given more than five years after the first broadcast of the contribution will entitle the contributor to receive the full original fee again, if the whole contribution is used.

School Cassettes

There is no agreement with the BBC for the use of talks contributions on cassette. (This means that the writer must negotiate his own agreement.)

Broadcast Use of Published Material

Domestic Radio

Plays	£7.95 per minute
Prose	£7.95 per minute
Poems	£7.95 per half minute
Prose for dramatisation	£6.20 per minute

World Service

Plays	£3.80 per minute
Prose	£3.80 per minute
Poems	£3.80 per half minute
Prose for dramatisation	£2.85 per minute

Foreign Language Service
One fifth of the rate paid for the World Service.

Radio 3 Continuity Readings
Paid for at the full prose rate — 7.95 per minute

Schools Cassettes
The BBC will pay 10% of the initial fee (or the current fee if the rights are taken up after the school year in which the work is first transmitted) for distribution of educational programmes on cassette. The 10% payment covers batches of 500 cassettes, so that a further payment becomes payable on the sale of the 501st, 1001st cassette and so on.

Unpublished Short Stories

These rates applied by the BBC are not negotiated by the unions:

	15'00	20'00
1st and 2nd stories	£82.00	£109.00
3rd, 4th and 5th stories	£94.00	£124.00
6th story	£107.00	£143.00

Local radio

In local radio producers will usually negotiate fees directly with a contributor. You may be offered nothing at all beyond charming thanks, cash in the hand to cover expenses when you come to the studio, or a T-shirt with the station logo. You may get a formal contract, probably after your contribution has been broadcast. It is up to you to be as business-like as you choose, and to balance the experience of broadcasting and having your material used against the value you place on your time.

Audio-visual scripts

If you become involved in the business world of writing promotional tape-slide scripts, your fee will depend on what the market can stand. You will need to assess how long a particular job will take you, and quote a fee based on a reasonable hourly or daily rate. Be realistic; think in terms of what sort of annual income you aim to earn, and base your fee on a proportion of this figure. There are no guide-lines.

Submitting a script or an idea

You will have gathered from other chapters in this book that there are many different sorts of radio script. If you have an idea for a talk in a magazine programme such as *Woman's Hour*, the best line of approach is to have it typed out and send it to the editor. You may be telephoned by a producer. The telephone conversation can be a sort of audition, to give the producer some idea of what you sound like, and an impression of your vocal personality. You can, if you like, send a cassette with your script, for the same purpose.

In the case of a larger project, perhaps an idea for a feature or a light entertainment series, it is best to approach a producer with a letter of enquiry and a synopsis before putting in a lot of work. If your idea is liked you may be encouraged to develop it more fully.

A newcomer is unlikely to be commissioned to write a full-length drama on the basis of a synopsis and a few pages of dialogue, so if your ambition is to write radio plays you had better submit a complete one. 'They' may not like it, but if they think you have potential you may be asked to write something else.

Scripts should be typed, in double spacing, with wide margins, on one side of the page only, preferably on A4 paper. There should be a front page with your name, address and telephone number, and this should be repeated on the last page, with the international copyright symbol. Fasten the script together with a staple or a brass paper-clip in the top left-hand corner. If it is bulky you can put it in a manila folder, but don't embed it in fancy binding. Attach a brief covering letter and send it with an envelope bearing return postage to your chosen destination. Don't forget to keep a copy.

Covering letters should be brief and to the point. If you have a track record, in radio or any other writing field, say so, but don't include an autobiography. Something like this will do:

The Script Editor
BBC Radio Drama
Broadcasting House
London W1A 1AA

Dear Sir,

I enclose the script of a 45-minute play which I hope may be suitable for *Afternoon Theatre*. The action takes place in Timbuktu, where I lived for some years.

Several short stories and a novel of mine have been published, but this is my first attempt at writing for radio.

Yours faithfully

Phyllida Borrett-Pickles

The first sentence alone would constitute a perfectly adequate covering letter.

It is a good idea to enclose also a stamped self-addressed postcard on which the company can acknowledge receipt of the typescript. The BBC usually does so, but not everyone is so scrupulous, and it is comforting to have proof that your script actually arrived as you settle down to wait for a response.

How long should you expect to wait? On average up to three months. If after that time you have heard nothing you can reasonably send a written enquiry. Don't telephone. Hopeless scripts get rejected more promptly than promising ones, and no news can be good news.

Persistence

Finally, the most valuable quality any writer can have in breaking into a new market is persistence. If at first you don't succeed, try, try again – and again. Be ruthless in analysing why your first submission was rejected. Put it away for six months and write something else. Then have a fresh look at the first effort, and see if the lapse of time has given you some new insights. And when you do succeed, keep up the pressure. You have a foot in the door of a highly competitive business, and people will forget all about you if you don't keep reminding them. Persistence and staying power win through in the end. Good luck!

Appendix I: Booklist

Reference and general interest

The History of Broadcasting in the United Kingdom (4 vols), Asa Briggs (OUP)

BBC Annual Report and Handbook 1987 (BBC)

Television and Radio 1987 (annual report and handbook) (IBA)

Broadcasting in America, Sydney W. Head (Houghton Mifflin Company 3rd edition 1976)

Broadcasting in Africa, edited by Sydney W. Head (Temple University Press 1974)

The Media in Britain, Jeremy Tunstall (Constable 1983)

Making the News, Peter Golding and Philip Elliott (Longman 1979)

Bad News, Glasgow Media Group (Routledge, Kegan Paul 1976)

World Radio-TV Handbook, edited by J.M. Frost (Billboard Publications, published annually)

A Microphone and a Frequency, Forty years of Forces Broadcasting, Doreen Taylor (Heinemann 1983)

Radio Luxembourg 1979 (Radio Luxembourg 1979)

BBC Features, edited by Laurence Gilliam (Evans/BBC 1950)

Around the World in 25 Years, Johnny Morris (Michael Joseph 1983)

Forever Ambridge: 30 years of the Archers, Norman Painting (Michael Joseph/BBC 1980)

The Archers: the first Thirty Years, edited by William Smethurst (Eyre Methuen 1980)

The Archers, a Slice of my Life, Godfrey Baseley (Sidgwick & Jackson 1971)

The Inside Story of Dick Barton, Geoffrey Webb, edited by Neil Tuson (Convoy Publications 1950)

Everything but Alf Garnett: A Personal View of BBC School Broadcasting, Kenneth Fawdry (BBC 1974)

BBC Children's Hour: A Celebration of those Magical Years, Wallace Grevatt (The Book Guild Ltd of Lewes 1988)

Goodnight Children, Everywhere, Ian Hartley (Midas Books 1983)

Chatterboxes: My Friends the Commentators, Brian Johnson (Methuen 1983)

How to do it

Writers' and Artists' Yearbook (A & C Black, published annually)

Research for Writers, Ann Hoffmann (A & C Black 1986)
The Way to Write Radio Drama, William Ash (Elm Tree Books 1985)
The Art of Radio, Donald McWhinnie (Faber 1959)
How to Write Comedy, Brad Ashton (Elm Tree Books)
Get It On, a Practical Guide to Getting Airtime, Jane Drinkwater (Pluto Press 1984)
Becoming a Writer, Dorothea Brande (Papermac 1983)
How Plays are Made, Stuart Griffiths (Heinemann Educational 1982)
The Complete Plain Words, Sir Ernest Gowers, revised by Sidney Greenbaum and Janet Whitcut (HMSO 1986)
The Spoken Word, a BBC Guide, Robert Burchfield (BBC 1981)
Writing for the BBC (BBC revised edition 1983)
Notes on Radio Drama Leaflet available on request from BBC Radio Drama Script Unit.
Writing for BBC Radio Light Entertainment Leaflet available on request from BBC Radio Light Entertainment Department.

Some published scripts

Postscripts 1940, J.B. Priestley (Heinemann 1940)
The Man Born to be King, a play cycle written on the life of our Lord and Saviour Jesus Christ, Dorothy L. Sayers (Gollancz 1943)

Six Plays for Radio:
  Mathry Beacon
  *The Disagreeable Oyster**
  Without the Grail
  *Under the Loofah Tree**
  Unman Wittering and Zigo
  Before the Monday   Giles Cooper (BBC 1966)

Best Radio Plays of 1978:
  Is it Something I said? Richard Harris
  Episode on a Thursday Evening, Don Haworth
  Remember Me, Jill Hyem
  Halt! Who goes there? Tom Mallin
  Daughters of Men, Jennifer Phillips
  Polaris, Fay Weldon   (Methuen)

Best Radio Plays of 1979:
  Typhoid Mary, Shirley Gee
  I never killed my German, Carey Harrison
  Heaven Scent, Barrie Keeffe
  Coxcomb, John Kirkmorris
  Attard in Retirement, John Peacock
  The Child, Olwen Wymark   (Methuen)

Best Radio Plays of 1981:
  The Jumping Mimuses of Byzantium, Peter Barnes

Talk of Love and War, Don Haworth
Family Voices, Harold Pinter
Beef, David Pownall
The Dead Image, J.P. Rooney
The Biggest Sandcastle in the World, Paul Thain   (Methuen)

Best Radio Plays of 1982:
Watching the Plays Together, Rhys Adrian
The Old Man Sleeps Alone, John Arden
Hoopoe Day, Harry Barton
Invisible Writing, Donald Chapman
The Dog It Was That Died, Tom Stoppard
Autumn Sunshine, William Trevor   (Methuen)

Best Radio Plays of 1983:
Time Slip, Wally K. Daly
Never in My Lifetime, Shirley Gee
The Angels They Grow Lonely, Gerry Jones
No Exceptions, Steve May
Scouting for Boys, Martyn Read   (Methuen)

Best Radio Plays of 1984:
Who is Sylvia? Steven Dunstone
Transfigured Night, Robert Ferguson
Daybreak, Don Haworth
The Wasted Years, Caryl Phillips
Swimmer, Christopher Russell
Temporary Shelter, Rose Tremain   (Methuen)

Best Radio Plays of 1985:
Outpatient, Rhys Adrian
King Canute, Barry Collins
Three Attempted Acts, Martin Crimp
Ploughboy Monday, David Pownall
Menocchio, James Saunders
Hiroshima: The Movie, Michael Wall   (Methuen)

*The Goon Show Scripts,** Spike Milligan (Woburn Press 1972)
*More Goon Show Scripts,** Peter Sellers, Harry Secombe and Spike Milligan
(Woburn Press 1973, Sphere 1974)
The ITMA Years, scripts broadcast between 1939 and 1949, Ted Kavanagh
(Woburn Press 1974, Futura 1975)
*Round the Horne,** Barry Took and Marty Feldman (Woburn Press 1974)

*Cassette tapes available. See below.

Cassette tapes and records

The BBC is developing a new policy on selling sound cassettes of
broadcast programmes. Many more are likely to be available in future. A
major step is the marketing of the whole of Radio 4's production of *Lord of*

the Rings. A copy of the current catalogue of BBC records and tapes can be obtained from

BBC Enterprises Ltd.,
Woodlands
80 Wood Lane
London W12 0TT

In ordering records or cassettes be clear whether you are being offered an original radio programme, or the sound-track of a television broadcast.

School radio programmes are not marketed by BBC Enterprises, but through the BBC Radio Shop, catalogue available from

BBC School Radio Information Office
1 Portland Place
London W1A 1AA

Appendix II:
Some Useful Addresses

British Broadcasting Corporation (BBC)

BBC
Broadcasting House, London W1A 1AA
Tel: 01–580–4468

BBC External Broadcasting
PO Box 76, Bush House, Strand, London WC2B 4PH
Tel: 01–240–3456

BBC Enterprises Ltd.
Woodlands, 80 Wood Lane, London W12 0TT
Tel: 01–743–5588

BBC Radio Shop
School Radio Information Office, 1 Portland Place, London W1A 1AA

BBC Radio Scotland
5 Queen Street, Edinburgh EH2 1JF
Tel: 031–225–3131

Broadcasting House
Beechgrove Terrace, Aberdeen AB9 2ZT
Tel: 0224–635233

12/13 Dock Street, Dundee
Tel: 0382–25025/259905

BBC Highland
7 Culduthel Road, Inverness IV2 4AD
Tel: 0463–221711

BBC Radio nan Gaidheal (Radio nan Eilean)
Rosebank, Church Street, Stornoway
Tel: 0851–5000

BBC Radio Solway
Elmbank, Lovers' Walk, Dumfries, DG1 1NZ
Tel: 0387–68008/9

BBC Radio Tweed
Municipal Buildings, High Street, Selkirk, TD7 4BU
Tel: 0750–21884

Queen Margaret Drive, Glasgow G12 8DG
Tel: 041–339–8844

BBC Radio Ulster
Broadcasting House, Ormeau Avenue, Belfast BT2 8HQ
Tel: 0232–244400

BBC Radio Wales/Radio Cymru
Broadcasting House, Llandaff, Cardiff CF5 2YQ
Tel: 0222 564888

Broadcasting House, Meirion Road, Bangor, Gwynedd LL57 2BY
Tel: 0792 54986

32 Alexandra Road, Swansea
Tel: 0792–54986

BBC Radio Clwyd, The Old School House, Glanrafon Road, Mold, Clwyd
Tel: 0352–59111

BBC Radio Gwent, Powys House, Cwmbran, Gwent
Tel: 06333 72727

BBC Network Production Centres

Birmingham: Broadcasting Centre, Pebble Mill Road, Birmingham B5 7QQ
Tel: 021–472–5353

Bristol: Broadcasting House, Whiteladies Road, Bristol BS8 2LR
Tel: 0272–32211

Manchester: New Broadcasting House, PO Box 27, Oxford Road,
Manchester M60 1SJ
Tel: 061–236–8444

Newcastle: Broadcasting House
54 New Bridge Street, Newcastle upon Tyne, NE1 8AA
Tel: 0632 320961

Elstree Centre
Clarendon Road, Borehamwood, Herts, WD6 1JF
Tel: 01–953–6100

Other BBC Regional Addresses

St Catherine's Close, All Saints Green, Norwich NR1 3ND
Tel: 0603–619331

South Western House, Canute Road, Southampton SO9 1PF
Tel: 0703–226201

Broadcasting House, Seymour Road, Mannamead, Plymouth PL3 5BD

Wilson House
Derby Road, Notttingham N91 5HX
Tel: 0602 472395

Broadcasting Centre
Woodhouse Lane, Leeds, LS2 9PX
Tel: 0532 41181/8

BBC Overseas Offices

USA: 630 Fifth Avenue, New York, NY., 10111, USA
Tel: 212–581–7100

Canada: Suite 1220, Manulife Centre, 55 Bloor Street West, Toronto, Ontario
Tel: 925–3891

Cairo Bureau: Flat 42, Kasr el Nil Street, PO Box 2040, Cairo, Egypt
Tel: Cairo 745898 and 748040

South East Asia Bureau: PO Box 434, Maxwell Road Post Office, Singapore
Tel: Singapore 9008

South America Office: Casilla de Correo, 1566 Buenos Aires, Argentina
Tel: 3926439

Australia and New Zealand: Westfield Towers, 100 William Street, Sydney, NSW 2011, Australia
Tel: Sydney 3586411

India: 1 Nizamuddin East, New Delhi 110013
Tel: 616108

France: 155 Rue du Faubourg Saint-Honoré, BP 487 08, 75366 Paris Cedex 08
Tel: 561 9700

Germany: BBC Bureau, 1 Berlin 12, Savignyplatz 6, W. Germany
Tel: West Berlin 316773, 316263

Belgium: PO Box 50, International Press Centre, 1041 Brussels
Tel: Brussels 736 8015

BBC Local Radio Stations

BBC Radio Bedfordshire
PO Box 476, Hastings Street, Luton, Bedfordshire, LU1 5BA
Tel: 0582–45911

BBC Radio Bristol
3 Tyndalls Park Road, Bristol, BS8 1PP
Tel: 0272–741111

BBC Radio Cambridgeshire
Broadcasting House, Hills Road, Cambridge, CB2 1LD
Tel: 0223–315970

BBC Radio Cleveland
Broadcasting House, Newport Road, Middlesbrough, Cleveland, TS1 5DG
Tel: 0642–225211

BBC Radio Cornwall
Phoenix Wharf, Truro, Cornwall TR1 1UA
Tel: 0872–75421

BBC Radio Cumbria
Hilltop Heights, London Road, Carlisle, Cumbria CA1 2NA
Tel: 0228–31661

BBC Radio Furness
Broadcasting House, Hartington Street, Barrow-in-Furness, Cumbria LA14
5SH
Tel: 02229–36767

BBC Radio Derby
56 St Helen's Street, Derby DE1 3HY
Tel: 0332–361111

BBC Radio Devon
St David's Hill, Exeter, Devon EX4 4DB
Tel: 0392–215651

BBC Essex
198 New London Road, Chelmsford, Essex CM2 9AB
Tel: 0245–262393

BBC Radio Humberside
63 Jameson Street, Hull HU1 3NU
Tel: 0482–23232

BBC Radio Kent
Sun Pier, Chatham, Kent ME4 4EZ
Tel: 0634–46284

BBC Radio Lancashire
King Street, Blackburn, Lancashire BB2 2EA
Tel: 0254–62411

BBC Radio Leeds
Broadcasting House, Woodhouse Lane, Leeds LS2 9PN
Tel: 0532–442131

BBC Radio Leicester
Epic House, Charles Street, Leicester LE1 3SH
Tel: 0533–27113

BBC Radio Lincolnshire
Radio Buildings, Newport, Lincoln LN1 3DF
Tel: 0522–40011

BBC Radio London
35a Marylebone High Street, London W1A 4LG
Tel: 01–486–7611

BBC Radio Manchester
New Broadcasting House, Oxford Road, Manchester M60 1SJ
Tel: 061–228–3434

BBC Radio Merseyside
55 Paradise Street, Liverpool L1 3BP
Tel: 051–708–5500

BBC Radio Newcastle
Broadcasting Centre, Barrack Road, Fenham, Newcastle-upon-Tyne NE99 1RN
Tel: 091—281—4243

BBC Radio Norfolk
Norfolk Tower, Surrey Street, Norwich NR1 3PA
Tel: 0603—617411

BBC Radio Northampton
Abington Street, Northampton, N1 2BE
Tel: 0604—20621

BBC Radio Nottingham
York House, Mansfield Road, Nottingham NG1 3JB
Tel: 0602—415161

BBC Radio Oxford
242/254 Banbury Road, Oxford OX2 7DW
Tel: 0865—53411

BBC Radio Sheffield
Ashdell Grove, 60 Westbourne Road, Sheffield S10 2QU
Tel: 0742—686185

BBC Radio Shropshire
2/4 Boscobel Drive, Shrewsbury, Shropshire SY1 3TT
Tel: 0743—248484

BBC Radio Solent
South Western House, Canute Road, Southampton SO9 4PJ
Tel: 0703—31311

BBC Radio Stoke-on-Trent
Conway House, Cheapside, Hanley, Stoke-on-Trent, Staffordshire ST1 1JJ
Tel: 0782—24827

BBC Radio Sussex
Marlborough Place, Brighton, Sussex BN1 1TU
Tel: 0273—680231

BBC Radio West Midlands
Pebble Mill Road, Birmingham B5 7SD
Tel: 021—472—5141

BBC Radio York
20 Bootham Row, York YO3 7BR
Tel: 0904—641351

Channel Islands

BBC Radio Guernsey
Commerce House, Les Banques, St Peter Port, Guernsey
Tel: 0481—28977

BBC Radio Jersey
Broadcasting House, Rouge Bouillon, St Helier, Jersey
Tel: 0534—70000

Independent Broadcasting

Independent Broadcasting Authority (IBA)
70 Brompton Road, London SW3 1EY
Tel: 01–584–7011

Association of Independent Radio Contractors (AIRC)
Regina House, 259–269 Old Marylebone Road, London NW1 5RA
Tel: 01–262–6681

Independent Radio News (IRN)
Communications House, Gough Square, London EC4P 4LP

Independent Radio Drama Productions Ltd.
65 Livingstone Road, London E17 9AU
Tel: 01–521–7384

Independent Local Radio Stations

Radio Aire (Leeds):
PO Box 362, Leeds LS3 1LR
Tel: 0532–452299

Beacon Radio (Wolverhampton and Black Country):
PO Box 303, Wolverhampton WV6 0DO
Tel: 0902–757211

BRMB Radio (Birmingham):
Radio House, PO Box 555, Ashton Road North, Birmingham B6 4BX
Tel: 021–359–4481/9

Radio Broadland (Great Yarmouth and Norwich):
St Georges Plain, 47/49 Colegate, Norwich NR3 1DD
Tel: 0603–630621

Capital Radio (London):
Euston Tower, London NW1 3DR
Tel: 01–388–1288

Chiltern Radio (Luton/Bedford)
Chiltern Road, Dunstable, LU6 1HQ
Tel: 0582–666001

55 Goldington Road, Bedford, MK40 3LS
Tel: 0234–49266

Radio City (Liverpool):
PO Box 194, Liverpool L69 1LD
Tel: 051–227–5100

Radio Clyde (Glasgow):
Clydebank Business Park, Clydebank, Glasgow G81 2RX
Tel: 041–941–1111

County Sound Radio (Guildford)
The Friary, Guildford GU1 4YX
Tel: 0483–505566

Devonair (Exeter/Torbay):
35/37 St David's Hill, Exeter, EX4 4DA
Tel: 0392—30703

Downtown Radio (Belfast/Londonderry):
Newtownards, County Down, Northern Ireland BT23 4ES
Tel: 0247—815555

Essex Radio (Southend/Chelmsford):
Radio House, Cliftown House, Southend-on-Sea SS1 1SX
Tel: 0702—333711

Radio House, 53 Duke Street, Chelmsford, Essex CM1 1SX
Tel: 0245—51141

Radio Forth (Edinburgh):
Forth House, Forth Street, Edinburgh EH1 3LF
Tel: 031—556—9255

GWR Radio (Bristol/Swindon/West Wiltshire);
PO Box 2000, Bristol BS99 7EX
Tel: 0272—279900

PO Box 2000, Swindon SN4 7EX
Tel: 0793—853222

Radio Hallam (Sheffield & Rotherham/Barnsley/Doncaster):
PO Box 194, Hartshead, Sheffield S1 1GP
Tel: 0742—766766

Hereward Radio (Peterborough and Northampton):
PO Box 225, Bridge Street, Peterborough PE1 1XI
Tel: 0733 46225

PO Box 1557, Abington Street, Northampton, NN1 2HW
Tel: 0604—29811

Invicta Radio (Maidstone and Medway/East Kent):
15 Station Road East, Canterbury, CT1 2RB
Tel: 0227 67661

37 Earl Street, Maidstone, ME14 1PF
Tel: 0622—679061

LBC News Radio (London):
Communications House, Gough Square, London EC4P 4LP
Tel: 01—353—1010

Leicester Sound (Leicester):
Granville House, Granville Road, Leicester LE1 7RW
Tel: 0533—551616

Marcher Sound (Wrexham and Deeside):
The Studios, Mold Road, Gwersyllt, Wrexham, Clwyd LL1 4AF
Tel: 0978—752202

Mercia Sound (Coventry):
Hertford Place, Coventry CV1 3TT
Tel: 0203—28451

Radio Mercury (Reigate and Crawley):

Broadfield House, Brighton Road, Crawley, West Sussex RH11 9TT
Tel: 0293–519161

Metro Radio (Tyne and Wear):
Newcastle-upon-Tyne NE99 1BB
Tel: 091–488 3131

Moray Firth Radio (Inverness):
PO Box 271, Inverness IV3 6SF
Tel: 0463–224433

Northsound Radio (Aberdeen):
45 King's Gate, Aberdeen AB2 6BL
Tel: 0224–632234

Ocean Sound (Portsmouth/Southampton):
Whittle Avenue, Segensworth West, Fareham, Hants PO15 5PA
Tel: 0489–589911

Radio Orwell (Ipswich):
Electric House, Lloyds Avenue, Ipswich IP1 3HZ
Tel: 0473–216971

Pennine Radio (Bradford/Huddersfield and Halifax):
Pennine House, 39 Well Street, Forster Square, Bradford BD1 5NP
Tel: 0274–731521

Piccadilly Radio (Manchester):
127/131 The Plaza, Piccadilly Plaza, Manchester M1 4AW
Tel: 061–236–9913

Plymouth Sound (Plymouth):
Earl's Acre, Plymouth PL3 4HX
Tel: 0752–227272

Red Dragon Radio (Cardiff/Newport):
Radio House, West Canal Wharf, Cardiff CF1 5XI
Tel: 0222–384041

Red Rose Radio (Preston and Blackpool):
PO Box 301, St Paul's Square, Preston PR1 1YE
Tel: 0772–556301

Saxon Radio (Bury St Edmunds):
Long Brackland, Bury St Edmunds, Suffolk IP3 1IY
Tel: 0284–701511

Severn Sound (Gloucester and Cheltenham):
PO Box 388, 67 Southgate Street, Gloucester GL1 2DQ
Tel: 0452–423791

Signal Radio (Stoke-on-Trent):
Studio 257, Stoke Road, Stoke-on-Trent ST4 2SR
Tel: 0782–417111

Southern Sound (Brighton):
Radio House, Franklin Road, Portslade, East Sussex BN4 2SS
Tel: 0273–422288

Swansea Sound (Swansea):
Victoria Road, Gowerton, Swansea SA4 3AB
Tel: 0792–893751/6

Radio Tay (Dundee/Perth):
PO Box 123, Dundee DD1 9UF
Tel: 0382–29551

Radio Tees (Teesside):
74 Dovecot Street, Stockton on Tees, Cleveland TS18 1HB
Tel: 0642–615111

Radio Trent (Nottingham):
29/31 Castle Gate, Nottingham NG1 7AP
Tel: 0602–581731

Two Counties Radio (Bournemouth):
5/7 Southcote Road, Bournemouth BH1 3LR
Tel: 0202–294881

Radio 210 (Reading):
PO Box 210, Reading, Berkshire RG3 5RZ
Tel: 0734–413131

Viking Radio (Humberside):
Commercial Road, Hull, North Humberside HU1 2SG
Tel: 0482–25141

West Sound (Ayr):
Radio House, Holmston Road, Ayr KA7 3BE
Tel: 0292–283662

Radio Wyvern (Hereford/Worcester):
5/6 Barbourne Terrace, Worcester WR1 3IS
Tel: 0905–612212

Overseas Radio Companies

Australia

Australian Broadcasting Corporation, Box 9994, Sydney, NSW, 2001
Manager for Europe: 54 Portland Place, London W1N 4DY

STW Channel 9, Swan Television and Radio Broadcasters Ltd., PO Box 99,
Tuart Hill, Western Australia 6060
Tel: 349 9999

Canada

Canadian Broadcasting Corporation, PO Box 500, Station 'A', Toronto,
M5W 1E6, Ontario
Tel: 416 925 3311

Canadian Radio-Television and Telecommunications Commission, Ottawa,
Ontario, K1A 0N2 Tel: 819 997 0313 (The federal authority which
regulates telecommunications and the broadcasting system in Canada)

India

All India Radio, Broadcasting House, Parliament Street, New Delhi, 110 001 is a part of the Ministry of Information and Broadcasting of the Government of India which operates the broadcasting network of the country. There are 90 centres covering almost the entire area of the country and catering for the various social, cultural and linguistic needs of the people.

The *External Services Division* of All India Radio broadcasts programmes in 25 languages. Programmes consist of news, daily commentary and press review, talks interviews, discussions and music, mainly Indian (classical, light, film and folk). These are broadcast in two major services: General Overseas Service in English, and the Urdu Service. The West Asian Service broadcasts programmes in Arabic, Dari, Persian, Pushtu and Baluchi. East African countries are serviced by the Swahili Service. The French Service is directed to South East Asia and North West Africa. Other area-oriented services are in Russian, Burmese, Chinese, Indonesian, Sinhala, Thai, Nepali and Tibetan languages. For Indians abroad there are services in Bengali, Gujarati, Hindi, Konkani, Punjabi, Sindhi, Tamil and Urdu. The object of these programmes is to entertain Indians abroad and keep them in touch with events and developments in India. There is also a special weekly programme for ethnic Indians in the USA, Canada and the UK.

Programmes for youth are broadcast from many stations of All India Radio. This service is mainly for the youth by the youth.

The *commercial service*, introduced first from AIR Bombay-Pune-Nagpur is now being broadcast on 31 AIR stations.

Ireland

Radio Telefis Eireann, Donnybrook, Dublin 4
Tel: 693111
The Irish national broadcasting service operating radio and television.

Radio talks and short stories (length 14 minutes) in Irish or English, features, dramatic or narrative and plays are welcomed and paid for according to merit. Plays should run 30, 60 or 90 minutes. Guidelines on writing for radio are available. MSS should be adressed to: RTE Radio 1, Radio Centre, Donnybrook, Dublin 4.

Luxembourg

Radio-Tele Luxembourg, Villa Louvigny, Luxembourg Ville
London Office: Radio Luxembourg (London) Ltd., 38 Hertford Street, London W1Y 8BA

New Zealand

Broadcasting Corporation of New Zealand, PO Box 98, Wellington
Tel: 04 721 777
Operates Radio and Television New Zealand.
Radio New Zealand, PO Box 2092, Wellington, Cl.
Tel: 04 741 555
A 24 hour service controlling three public radio networks (one commercial)

and also a limited shortwave service directed primarily to the Southwest Pacific Islands and Southeastern Australia.

South Africa

South African Broadcasting Corporation, PO Box 8606, Johannesburg 2000
Tel: 714 9118
Operates five national networks: Radio South Africa, Radio Suid-Afrika, Radio 5, Radio Orion, and Radio Allegro; and seven regional services: Radio Highveld, Radio Port Natal, Radio Good Hope, Radio Lotus, Radio Jacarabda, Radio Algoa, Radio Oranje. Also the nine radio services in Ngun and Sotho languages broadcast in Zulu, Xhosa, Southern Sotho, Northern Sotho, Tswana, Venda, Tsonga, Swazi and Ndebele.

In 1966 the SABC introduced an *External Service* known as RSA The Voice of South Africa. This broadcasts to all corners of the world in eleven languages – English, Afrikaans, Portuguese, French, German, Dutch, ChiChewa, Swahili, Lozi, Tsonga and Spanish.

There are openings for plays, feature programmes, talks, short stories, light entertainment and youth and children's programmes. Outside contributors should remember that Radio South Africa caters for a South African public, with its own needs, ideas and tastes.

United States of America

American Broadcasting Company, ABC News, 8 Carburton Street, London W1P 7DT
Tel: 01 637 9222
CBS News, European Broadcast Centre, 68 Knightsbridge, London SW1X 7LL
Tel: 01 581 4801
NBC News Worldwide Inc., 8 Bedford Avenue, London WC1B 3NQ
Tel: 01 637 8655

Miscellaneous

BBC/Open University Production Centre:
Walton Hall, Milton Keynes, MK7 6BH
Tel: 0908 74033

British Forces Broadcasting Service (BFBS), PO Box 1234, North Wharf Road, London W2 1LA

TALC (Teaching Aids at Low Cost), PO Box 49, St Albans, Herts AL1 4AX

Graves Medical Audio-Visual Library, Holly House, 220 New London Road, Chelmsford CM2 9BJ
Tel: 0245 283351

Societies and Associations

National Association of Student Broadcasters (NASB), Norwich House, University of Sussex, Brighton BN1 9QS
Tel: 0273–698113 Ext. 24

Association of Talking Newspapers for the Blind (TNAUK), 68a High Street, Heathfield, East Sussex TN21 8JB

The Society of Authors, 84 Drayton Gardens, London SW10 9SB
Tel: 01–373–6642

The Writers Guild of Great Britain, 430 Edgware Road, London W2 1EH
Tel: 01–723–8074/5/6

The Radio Academy (a professional association for those involved in radio broadcasting)
2nd floor, Whiteladies Road, Bristol BS8 2LG
Tel: 0272–237485

Voice of the Listener (a non profit-making society to support the quality of sound and the spoken word in radio broadcasting)
101 Kings Drive, Gravesend, Kent DA12 5BQ
Tel: 0474–350304

Appendix III:

This Gun That I Have in My Right Hand is Loaded
by
Timothy West

ANNOUNCER: Midweek Theatre
(MUSIC and keep under:)
We present John Pullen and Elizabeth Proud as Clive and
Laura Barrington, Malcolm Hayes as Heinrich
Oppenheimer, Diana Olsson as Gerda, and Dorit Welles
as The Barmaid, with John Hollis, Anthony Hall and
Fraser Kerr, in *This Gun That I Have in My Right Hand is
Loaded* by Timothy West, adapted for radio by H. and
Cynthia Old Hardwick-Box.
This Gun That I Have in My Right Hand is Loaded
(BRING UP MUSIC THEN CROSSFADE TO TRAFFIC
NOISES. WIND BACKED BY SHIP'S SIRENS, DOG
BARKING, HANSOM CAB, ECHOING FOOTSTEPS,
KEY CHAIN, DOOR OPENING, SHUTTING)

LAURA: (*off*) Who's that?

CLIVE: Who do you think, Laura, my dear? Your husband.

LAURA: (*approaching*) Why, Clive!

RICHARD: Hello, Daddy.

CLIVE: Hello, Richard. My, what a big boy you're getting. Let's
see, how old are you now?

RICHARD: I'm six, Daddy.

LAURA: Now Daddy's tired, Richard, run along upstairs and I'll
call you when it's supper time.

RICHARD: All right, Mummy.
(RICHARD RUNS HEAVILY UP WOODEN STAIRS)

LAURA: What's that you've got under your arm, Clive?

CLIVE: It's an evening paper, Laura.
(PAPER NOISE)
I've just been reading about the Oppenheimer smuggling
case. (*effort noise*) Good gracious, it's nice to sit down
after that long train journey from the insurance office in
the City.

LAURA:	Let me get you a drink, Clive darling. (LENGTHY POURING, CLINK)
CLIVE:	Thank you, Laura, my dear. (CLINK, SIP, GULP) Aah! Amontillado, eh? Good stuff. What are you having?
LAURA:	I think I'll have a whisky, if it's all the same to you. (CLINK, POURING, SYPHON)
CLIVE:	Whisky, eh? That's a strange drink for an attractive auburn-haired girl of twenty nine. Is there . . . anything wrong?
LAURA:	No, it's nothing, Clive, I –
CLIVE:	Yes?
LAURA:	No, really, I –
CLIVE:	You're my wife, Laura. Whatever it is, you can tell me. I'm your husband. Why, we've been married – let me see – eight years, isn't it?
LAURA:	Yes, I'm sorry Clive, I . . . I'm being stupid. It's . . . just . . . this. (PAPER NOISE)
CLIVE:	This? Why, what is it, Laura?
LAURA:	It's . . . it's a letter. I found it this morning in the letter box. The Amsterdam postmark and the strange crest on the back . . . it . . . frightened me. It's addressed to you. Perhaps you'd better open it.
CLIVE:	Ah ha. (ENVELOPE TEARING AND PAPER NOISE) Oh, dash it, I've left my reading glasses at the office. Read it to me, will you, my dear.
LAURA:	Very well. (PAPER NOISE) Let's see. "Dear Mr Barrington. If you would care to meet me in the Lounge Bar of Berridge's Hotel at seven-thirty on Tuesday evening the twenty-first of May, you will hear something to your advantage. (CROSSFADE TO OPPENHEIMER'S VOICE AND BACK AGAIN IMMEDIATELY) Please wear a dark red carnation in your buttonhole for identification purposes. Yours faithfully, H.T. Oppenheimer." Clive! Oppenheimer! Surely that's –
CLIVE:	By George, you're right. Where's my evening paper. (PAPER NOISE AS BEFORE) Yes! Oppenheimer! He's the man wanted by the police in connection with this smuggling case.
LAURA:	Darling, what does it all mean?
CLIVE:	Dashed if I know. But I intend to find out. Pass me that Southern Region Suburban Timetable on the sideboard there. Now, where are we – (BRIEF PAPER NOISE)

Six fifty-one! Yes, I'll just make it. Lucky we bought those dark red carnations.
(FLOWER NOISE)
There we are. Well — (*stretching for fade*) — Lounge Bar of Berridge's Hotel, here . . . I . . . come. . . .
(FADE)
(FADE IN PUB NOISES. GLASSES, CHATTER, TILL, DARTS, SHOVE-HALFPENNY, HONKYTONK PIANO, KNEES UP MOTHER BROWN ETC.)

HAWKINS: (*middle-aged, cheerful, Londoner*) Evening, Mabel. Busy tonight, isn't it.

BARMAID: It certainly is, Mr Hawkins. I've been on my feet all evening. (*going off*) Now then, you lot, this is a respectable house, this is.
(SINGING AND PIANO FADES ABRUPTLY TO SILENCE)

FARRELL: (*approaching, middle-aged, cheerful, Londoner*) Evening, George, what are you having?

HAWKINS: No, no, let me.

FARRELL: Come on!

HAWKINS: Well, then, a pint of the usual.
(TILL)

FARRELL: Two pints of the usual, please, Mabel.
(MONEY)

BARMAID: (*off*) Coming up, Mr Farrell.

HAWKINS: Evening, Norman.

JACKSON: (*middle-aged, cheerful, Londoner*) Hello there George. What are you having, Bert?

FARRELL: I'm just getting them, Norman.

JACKSON: Well, leave me out then, I'm getting one for Charlie Illingworth. Two halves of the usual, Mabel.

BAINES: (*coming up, middle-aged, cheerful, Londoner*) Evening all.

JACKSON: Hello, Arnold, haven't seen you in ages.
(TILL)

BARMAID: Your change, Mr Farrell.
(MONEY)

FARRELL: Thanks Mabel. Where's Charlie got to? Ah, there you are. Charlie, you know Arnold Baines, don't you?

ILLING: (*cheerful, Londoner, middle-aged*) Known the old so-and-so for ages. What'll you have?

JACKSON: No, I'm getting them, what is it?

BAINES: Oh, I'll just have my usual, thanks.

JACKSON: Who's looking after you, George, old man?
(MONEY)

BARMAID: There's yours, Mr Hawkins.

HAWKINS: Bung ho.
(TILL)

FARRELL: Cheers George.

BAINES:	Cheers Norman.
JACKSON:	Cheers Bert.
ILLING:	Cheers Arnold.
	(TILL)
BAINES:	Well, well, look who's coming over.
ILLING:	Isn't that young Clive Barrington from the Providential Insurance?
BAINES:	As happily married a man as ever I saw.
CLIVE:	(*approach*) Evening Arnold. Evening Bert, Charlie, George. Evening Norman.
BARMAID:)	(Evening Mr Barrington.
FARRELL:)	(Evening Clive.
BAINES:)	(*simul.*) (Long time no see.
JACKSON:)	(Hallo Barrington old lad.
ILLING:)	(How goes it.
HAWKINS:)	(What ho then mate.
HAWKINS:	What are you having?
CLIVE:	A whisky, please.
HAWKINS:	Any particular brand?
CLIVE:	I'll have the one nearest the clock.
HAWKINS:	Half a minute. There's a bloke over there can't take his eyes off you, Clive. Over in the corner, see him? Wearing a dark blue single-breasted dinner jacket and tinted spectacles. A foreigner, or my name's not George Hawkins.
CLIVE:	Yes, by George, you're right, George. Excuse me. (PEAK CHATTER)
OPPENHEIMER:	(*middle-European accent*) So, Herr Barrington, you are here at last. I was becoming impatient.
CLIVE:	Well, now I am here, perhaps you would be so good as to explain what the blazes all this is about?
OPPEN:	Certainly, but not here. We will go to my place in Wiltshire where we can talk. My car is outside. Come. (FADE ON PUB BACKGROUND) (FADE UP CAR NOISE SLOWING, STOPPING, ENGINE TICKING OVER) Excuse me, Officer.
POLICEMAN:	Yes, Sir?
OPPEN:	Am I on the right road for Wiltshire?
POLICEMAN:	That's right sir. Straight on, then turn left. (CAR REVS UP, MOVES OFF, CROSSFADE TO CAR SLOWING DOWN ON GRAVEL PATH AND STOPPING. CAR DOOR BANGS EIGHT TIMES. FOOTSTEPS ON GRAVEL. FRONT DOOR CREAKS OPEN. DISTANT PIANO, MOONLIGHT SONATA)
OPPEN:	Ah, that is my sister playing. (PIANO NEARER. THE SONATA COMES TO ITS CLOSE. SUSPICION OF NEEDLE NOISE AT END)

GERDA:	Ha! Managed that difficult A flat major chord at last.
OPPEN:	Gerda, my dear, we have a visitor. Herr Clive Barrington from the Providential Insurance Gesellschaft. Herr Barrington, this is my sister Gerda.
GERDA:	I am pleased to meet you, Herr Barrington. Has Heinrich told you what we have in mind?
OPPEN:	Nein, not yet, Liebchen. Herr Barrington, first a drink. Champagne, I think, to celebrate.
	(CHAMPAGNE CORK, POUR, FIZZ, CLINK)
CLIVE:	Thank you. Now, Mr Oppenheimer, or whatever your name is, don't you think it's time you did some explaining?
OPPEN:	Ja, of course. The stolen diamonds about which your Major Kenwood-Smith has seen fit to call in Scotland Yard –
CLIVE:	Major Kenwood-Smith? You mean the Major Kenwood-Smith who's head of my department at the Insurance Office?
OPPEN:	Right first time, Herr Barrington. As I was saying, the diamonds are safely in my hands.
CLIVE:	What! You mean to tell me –
OPPEN:	One moment, please, let me continue. I intend to return them, but on one condition. Now listen carefully; this ... is ... what ... I ... want ... you ... to ... do. ...
	(FADE AND UP)
	... and I think that is all I need to tell you, my dear Herr. Now I must leave you: I have one or two ... little matters to attend to. (*on mike*) Auf wiedersehen.
	(DOOR SLAMS IMMEDIATELY SOME WAY OFF)
GERDA:	Won't you sit down, Herr Barrington.
CLIVE:	Thank you, Countess.
	(SITTING NOISE)
	Look, I don't know how far you're involved in this hellish business, but I would just like to say how exquisitely I thought you played that sonata just now. It happens to be a favourite of mine.
GERDA:	Ja? You liked my playing, yes?
CLIVE:	Beautiful, and yet ... no, it would be impertinent of me. ...
GERDA:	Please.
CLIVE:	Well then, if you insist. I thought that in the Andante – the slow movement – your tempo was a little ... what shall I say?
GERDA:	Strict?
CLIVE:	Exactly.
GERDA:	(*coming in close*) I had no idea you knew so much about music.
CLIVE:	Please, Countess, I beg of you. I don't know what kind

	of a hold that filthy swine your brother has over you, and I don't want to know, but you don't belong here. For Pete's sake, why not leave with me now, before it's too late.
GERDA:	Nein, nein, I cannot ... (*in tears*)
CLIVE:	Why, Countess, why?
GERDA:	I will tell you. It is better that you should know. It all started a long time ago, when I was a little Fraulein in the tiny village of Bad Obersturmmbannfeurhershof, in the Bavarian Alps. ... (FADE. BRING UP LONDON TRAFFIC. BIG BEN CHIMES THE HOUR AND THEN STRIKES TWELVE. AS IT STRIKES WE MOVE OUT OF THE TRAFFIC, A CAR STOPS, SQUEAL OF BRAKES, CAR DOORS, FOOTSTEPS, NEWSBOYS, TUGS, BARREL ORGAN, CREAKING DOOR, MORE FOOTSTEPS DOWN A VERY VERY LONG CORRIDOR PASSING OFFICES WITH TYPEWRITERS UNTIL A SMALL DOOR OPENS AT THE END OF THE PASSAGE AND WE MOVE INTO A SMALL ROOM ON THE LAST STROKE OF TWELVE)
POWELL:	Ha! Twelve o'clock already. Morning, Sergeant McEwan. Or perhaps I should say "Good Afternoon."
McEWAN:	(*Scots*) Whichever you like, sir! (GOOD HUMOURED LAUGHTER)
POWELL:	As a matter of fact, I've been out on a job already this morning. I bet you just thought I'd overslept, didn't you, Sergeant?
McEWAN:	What, you, sir? Hoots, no. Not Detective-Inspector 'Bonzo' Powell, V.C., who went over the top at Tobruk; one-time Channel swimmer, and one of the toughest, and at the same time one of the most popular, officers at Scotland Yard here? I should say not. Och.
POWELL:	No, I got a line on our old friend Heinrich Oppenheimer, at long last. Our chap at Swanage says Oppenheimer has a private submarine moored nearby — it's my guess he'll try and get the diamonds out of the country tonight.
McEWAN:	Havers! Where will he make for d'ye ken?
POWELL:	I don't know, but it's my guess he'll make straight for Amsterdam. Come on, Sergeant, we're going down to swanage. And ... the ... sooner ... the ... better. ... (URGENT MUSIC, THEN FADE BEHIND GULLS, ROWLOCKS, WASH. STUDIO CLOCK SHOULD BE PARTICULARLY NOTICEABLE IN THIS SCENE) (NOTE: ALL THE GERMANS IN THIS SCENE ARE INDISTINGUISHABLE ONE FROM THE OTHER, AND INDEED MAY ALL BE PLAYED BY THE SAME ACTOR AS OPPENHEIMER)

LUDWIG:	We are nearly at the submarine now, mein Kommandant.
OPPEN:	Ach. Zehr gut. Tell me once more what you have done with the prisoners; my sister Gerda and that meddling fool Barrington.
LUDWIG:	Karl found them attempting to telephone Scotland Yard from the porter's lodge. They have been tied up and taken on board the submarine half.an hour ago.
OPPEN:	That is gut. I will teach the fool Englishman to double cross me. Achtung! Here we are at the submarine. Karl! Heinz! Kurt! Lower a rope ladder!
KARL:	Ja, mein Kommandant. (FEET ON TIN TRAY)
OPPEN:	It is four o'clock. We will sail immediately. (CHANGE TO SUBMARINE INTERIOR ACCOUSTIC)
HEINZ:	The diamonds are safely locked in your cabin, mein Kommandant.
OPPEN:	Jawohl. Kurt! Heinz! Karl! Prepare to dive! (DIVING NOISES. KLAXON) Set a course for Amsterdam.
KURT:	Steer East North East eight degrees by north. (CRIES OF JAWOHL, ACHTUNG, MIDSHIPS etc.)
OPPEN:	Ludwig!
LUDWIG:	Ja, mein Kommandant.
OPPEN:	Take me to the prisoners.
LUDWIG:	Ja, mein Kommandant. (MORE FEET ON TIN TRAY) They are in the forward hydroplane compartment. (DOOR OPENS. FORWARD HYDROPLANE COMPARTMENT NOISES)
OPPEN:	So, Herr Barrington, we meet again.
CLIVE:	You filthy swine, Oppenheimer, you won't get away with this.
OPPEN:	(*becoming slightly manic*) On the contrary, my friend, there is no power on earth that can stop me now. You, I'm afraid, will never reach Amsterdam. There will be an unfortunate ... accident in the escape hatch.
GERDA:	(*a gasp*) Heinrich! You don't mean. ...
OPPEN:	As for you, my dear sister Gerda. ...
CLIVE:	Leave the girl out of it, Oppenheimer. She's done nothing to you.
OPPEN:	Charming chivalry, my English friend. But it is to no avail. Come.
CLIVE:	All right, you swine, you've asked for it! (BLOW)
OPPEN:	Aargh. Himmel! Karl, Kurt! (RUNNING FOOTSTEPS)
CLIVE:	Ah, would you? Then try *this* for size. (BLOW. GROAN)

	If *that*'s the way you want it.
	(BLOW. GROAN)
KURT:	Get him, Hans.
CLIVE:	Ah, no you don't. Take *that*.
	(BLOW. GROAN. A CHAIR FALLS OVER)
GERDA:	Look out, Clive. The one with glasses behind you. He's got a gun.
	(SHOT)
CLIVE:	(*winces*)
	(ANOTHER CHAIR FALLS OVER)
	Phew! Close thing, that.
GERDA:	Clive! What happened?
CLIVE:	Just my luck; he got me in the arm. Luckily, he caught his foot on that bulkhead coaming; he must have struck his head on that valve group between the depth gauge and the watertight torpedo door.
GERDA:	Is he − ?
CLIVE:	I'm afraid so. Right, now to get this thing surfaced.
GERDA:	Do you know how?
CLIVE:	It shouldn't be too difficult. Luckily I had a week on Subs in the R.N.V.R. years ago. (*with pain*) This right arm being Kaput doesn't help, though. Right, now, just blow ... the ... ballast from main ... and ... number four ... tanks ... adjust the Hammerschmidt-Brucke stabilisers ... and up − we − go.
	(SURFACING NOISES. SEA. THE CRY OF GULLS. A FEW BARS OF "DESERT ISLAND DISCS" MUSIC. CROSSFADE TO CHATTER, CLINK OF GLASSES)
LAURA:	Have another drink, Sergeant.
McEWAN:	Thank you, Mrs Barrington. I'll have a wee drappie.
CLIVE:	How about you, Inspector?
POWELL:	Don't mind if I do, sir. Charming place you have here, if I may say so; and a charming wife to go with it.
LAURA:	(*blushing*) Thank you, Inspector.
CLIVE:	Well, I don't mind saying, Inspector, there were one or two moments today when I wondered if I'd ever see either of them again.
LAURA:	Tell us, Inspector, exactly when was it you came to realise that Major Kenwood-Smith was behind it all?
POWELL:	Well, for a long time it had puzzled us that the safe was blown by a left-handed man − Oppenheimer and his henchmen are all right-handed. Luckily one of our chaps noticed Kenwood-Smith signing a cheque with his *left* hand.
CLIVE:	Aha.
POWELL:	We asked him a few questions, and he broke down and confessed. Sergeant, you can go on from there.
McEWAN:	Ay, well, the diamonds aboard the submarine turned out

	to be imitation. Oppenheimer must have been double-crossed at the last minute, and someone in Berridge's Hotel must have performed the switch.
CLIVE:	Great Scott, the barmaid!
POWELL:	Right, first time, Mr Barrington. We checked in our archives, and she turned out to have a record as long as your arm. She made a dash for it, but in the end she broke down and confessed.
CLIVE:	So everything turned out for the best in the end, eh?
POWELL:	That's right sir. And just think, Mrs Barrington, if it hadn't been for young Richard here losing his puppy on Wimbledon Common, none of this might ever have happened.
	(YAPPING ON DISC)
RICHARD:	Down, Lucky, down!
POWELL:	Now then, young pup, none of that gnawing at my trouser leg, or I'll have to take you into custody as well! (GENERAL LAUGHTER. LIGHT HEARTED ROUNDING-OFF MUSIC AND UP TO FINISH.)
ANNOUNCER:	*(spinning it out – the Play has under-run)*: You have been listening to *This Gun That I Have in My Right Hand is Loaded* . . .

Index